Wild Guide Calendar 2014

Wild Guide Calendar 2014

continued from page 1

WHAT IS WILDERNESS?

The Wilderness Act of 1964 established the National Wilderness Preservation System to preserve the last remaining wildlands in America. The Wilderness Act, as federal policy, secures an enduring resource of wilderness for the people. Wilderness is defined as an area that has primarily been affected by the forces of nature with the imprint of humans substantially unnoticeable. It is an area that offers outstanding opportunity for solitude or a primitive or unconfined type of recreation, and an area that contains ecological, geological, or other features of scientific, educational, scenic, or historical value.

New Mexico Wilderness Alliance/NM Wild
WILD GUIDE 2014

Editor: Tina Deines

Art Director/Designer: Paula Eastwood
www.eastwooddesignsf.com

Cartographer: Kerrie Bushway

Copy Editor: Tania Soussan

Front cover: Wilderness Act Anniversary Seal re-created from the original seal for the 50th anniversary of the first designated wilderness in 1924.

Back cover: Otero Mesa pronghorn antelope, courtesy of BLM/New Mexico.
Special thanks to all BLM/New Mexico employees who contributed photos to *Wild Guide 2014*.

Printed on recycled paper by Starline Printing, Albuquerque

For more copies of *Wild Guide 2014* contact Tina Deines, *tina@nmwild.org*.

MISSION STATEMENT
The New Mexico Wilderness Alliance/NM Wild is dedicated to the protection, restoration, and continued enjoyment of New Mexico's wildlands and Wilderness areas.

RIGHT: BUREAU OF LAND MANAGEMENT

Kayakers on the Rio Grande

Celebration. Responsibility. Momentum. Opportunity.

BY **MARK ALLISON,** Executive Director

I am very pleased to present to you the New Mexico Wilderness Alliance's Wild Guide 2014. Our primary purpose for this annual publication is to get you outside to personally experience wilderness. We know that is the very best path for people to become life-long advocates.

As in previous years, this guide is chock full of ideas and opportunities to help you explore the special wild places of the Land of Enchantment. In these pages, you'll find everything from guided rafting trips to llama hikes to overnight backpack trips in search of endangered Mexican gray wolves. As always, there are a number of stunning day hikes and service projects for all abilities led by NM Wild staff as well as practical tips for enjoying the outdoors when you are out on your own. We hope you'll join us and that these trips will provide you with the inspiration to get outside with your friends and family to discover the magnificent beauty of New Mexico's wilderness this year.

This is a very special year for us as 2014 marks the 50th anniversary of the Wilderness Act and the 90th anniversary of the world's first administratively-protected wilderness–our own Gila Wilderness. A highlight among our many anniversary activities will be the National Wilderness Conference from October 15-19 in Albuquerque. We are co-hosting this event and expect hundreds of people from all over the country to attend, which will provide us an excellent opportunity to showcase both our existing protected wilderness and our current campaigns to protect more.

New Mexico has a rich and proud legacy of protecting wild places. We played a central role in the creation and evolution of the wilderness protection movement itself. During this anniversary year, we want to remind ourselves why wilderness is essential, honor the vision and efforts of those who came before us and renew our commitment to preserve additional deserving lands now under threat.

Many of the things we most enjoy and associate with being outside while we are hiking, backpacking, hunting or fishing are available to us because of the additional and permanent protections afforded to federally designated wilderness areas. The solitude, the lack of commercial development, the absence of noise and fumes from off-road vehicles and chainsaws, the knowledge that oil and gas drilling are not allowed, clean air and water, wildlife–these things are a result of the 1964 Wilderness Act.

Unfortunately, despite our special history of being "first," today only 2 percent of our land area is federally protected wilderness, the smallest percentage of any of the 11 Western states. We at NM Wild see this as an opportunity and feel a sense of urgency. There are an estimated 4.6 million acres in New Mexico that are roadless and deserving of further investigation to determine if they would qualify for wilderness, including a number of the areas highlighted in these pages. Do your favorite places enjoy the permanent protections of designated wilderness? If not, they could be under threat and lost forever.

I am proud to be associated with such a smart, dedicated and persistent group of people working to protect New Mexico's wild places. We're going to do our very best to make sure that NM Wild is the strongest, most effective, homegrown, statewide, grassroots, membership advocacy group that we can be. We have big plans for the upcoming year and plan to use the momentum coming off of the recent victory protecting Rio Grande del Norte. Our chances for success will very much depend on growing and engaging our 5,000 members. Are you one?

There are lots of ways you can help NM Wild.

- Join or renew your membership.
- Ask your friends and family to join NM Wild.
- Give the 2014 Wild Guide as a gift to your loved ones.
- Join us for one of our many outings, including our winter trip to Yellowstone.
- Act on our advocacy alerts.
- Volunteer in the field or the office.
- Host a membership gathering.
- Write a piece for our newsletter.
- Contribute financially what you can.
- Let us know what is on your mind!

Thanks again for doing your part to protect wilderness. I look forward to working with you in 2014. Remember: *Celebration. Responsibility. Momentum. Opportunity.* See you on the trail!

Go to our website at *www.nmwild.org* to sign up for an adventure, get the latest news and find out how to join our collective voice for wilderness.

Table of Contents

BUREAU OF LAND MANAGEMENT

Hiking in the Organ Mountains

EXTRAS

People & Events —This Year with NM Wild

1. NM Wild hosts world-renowned pianist **Hélène Grimaud** for a concert benefiting Mexican gray wolves.
2. Las Cruces staffers host vets for a tour of WWII bombing targets within the **Organ Mountains-Desert Peaks** proposed national monument.
3. NM Wild staff, board and friends welcome new Executive Director **Mark Allison** and Gila Grassroots Organizer **Nathan Newcomer**.
4. Board Chair **Ken Cole** presents an award to Associate Director **Tisha Broska** for her extraordinary work in the past year.

John Olivas

MARK LELLOUCH

Emma Tomingas-Hatch with Sophia at Wolf Rally

Mark Allison, NM Wild Executive Director

4.

MARK LELLOUCH

Ken Salazar, former US Secretary of the Interior at the Rio Grande del Norte celebration

NEW MEXICO WILDERNESS ALLIANCE

P.O. Box 25464 Albuquerque, NM 87125 505-843-8696 505-843-8697 (fax)

www.nmwild.org

ALBUQUERQUE

Executive Director
Mark Allison

Associate Director
Tisha Broska

Finance Manager
Roxanne Pacheco

Communications Coordinator
Tina Deines

Staff Attorney
Judy Calman

Administrative Assistant
Emma Tomingas-Hatch

GIS Coordinator
Lynne Uhring

NORTHERN NEW MEXICO

Traditional Community Organizer
John Olivas

LAS CRUCES

Southern NM Director
Jeff Steinborn

Wilderness Protection Coordinator
Nathan Small

GILA REGION

Grassroots Coordinator
Nathan Newcomer

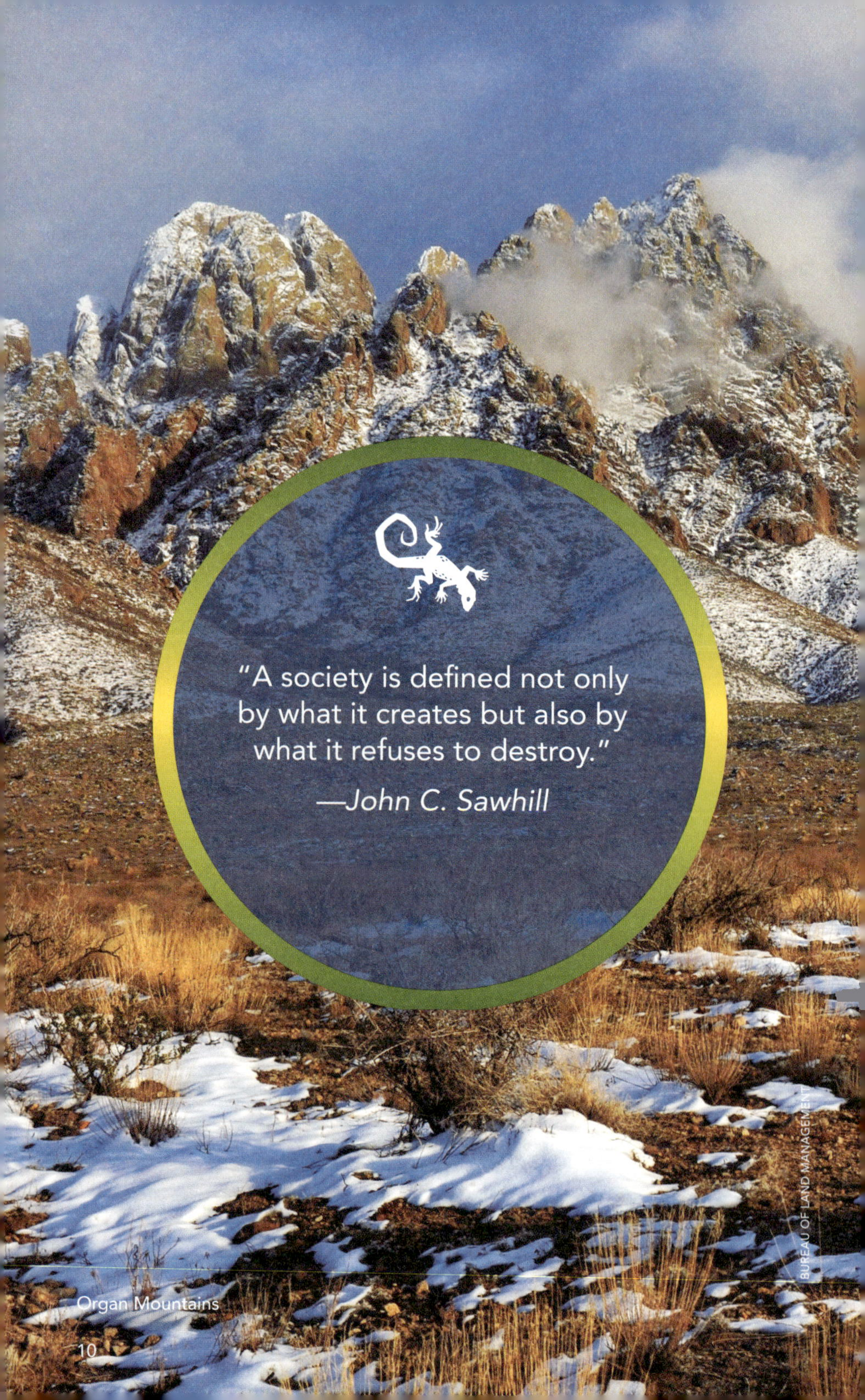

"A society is defined not only by what it creates but also by what it refuses to destroy."

—John C. Sawhill

Organ Mountains

BUREAU OF LAND MANAGEMENT

Wilderness Campaigns

RIO GRANDE DEL NORTE: Victory!

STAFF REPORT

On March 25, 2013, President Obama designated the Rio Grande del Norte (RGDN) National Monument in Northern New Mexico, protecting some 242,500 acres in Taos County, including the Taos Plateau, Ute Mountain and the Rio Grande Gorge.

New Mexico Wilderness Alliance (NM Wild) has been working to permanently protect this landscape since 2007 and the support of NM Wild members was critical to the campaign's success.

"We are thrilled that President Obama used his authority under the 1906 Antiquities Act to designate Rio Grande del Norte as a protected area, keeping it free of development," said John Olivas, traditional community organizer for NM Wild. "Many generations have enjoyed and lived off this landscape, and now President Obama has ensured the local community that this special place will stay as it is for our children, grandchildren and those who follow."

The section of the Rio Grande that flows through the RGDN was protected in 1968 under the National Wild and Scenic River System, and this new layer of protection as a national monument adds security to the land surrounding the river. The designation also safeguards hunting, fishing, grazing, wood gathering, and herb/piñon gathering.

Over the last two decades, supporters—including grazing permittees, Taos Pueblo leaders, land grant heirs, acequia parciantes and mayordomos, local businesses, elected officials and a host of individual supporters—have urged the New Mexico federal delegation to protect this landscape.

The Rio Grande del Norte includes rugged, wide open plains that average 7,000 feet in elevation, and is cut by steep canyons with rivers tucked away in their depths. The Río Grande carves a gorge cutting down 800 feet through layers of volcanic basalt flows and ash. The monument is also spotted with volcanic cones, including Ute Mountain at 10,093 feet

"This national monument designation will serve as a fitting legacy to retired Sen. Jeff Bingaman, a champion for conservation in New Mexico," Olivas said. "He introduced legislation to safeguard this area years ago and worked diligently with his colleagues to move it through Congress." Rep. Ben Ray Luján and Sens. Tom Udall and Martin Heinrich backed Bingaman's efforts through the years. "We are grateful for the swift action of President Obama to allow us to pass down this land and our traditions to future generations," Olivas added.

Esther Garcia, president of San Antonio del Rio Colorado Land Grant

RIGHT: BUREAU OF LAND MANAGEMENT

Rio Grande del Norte National Monument

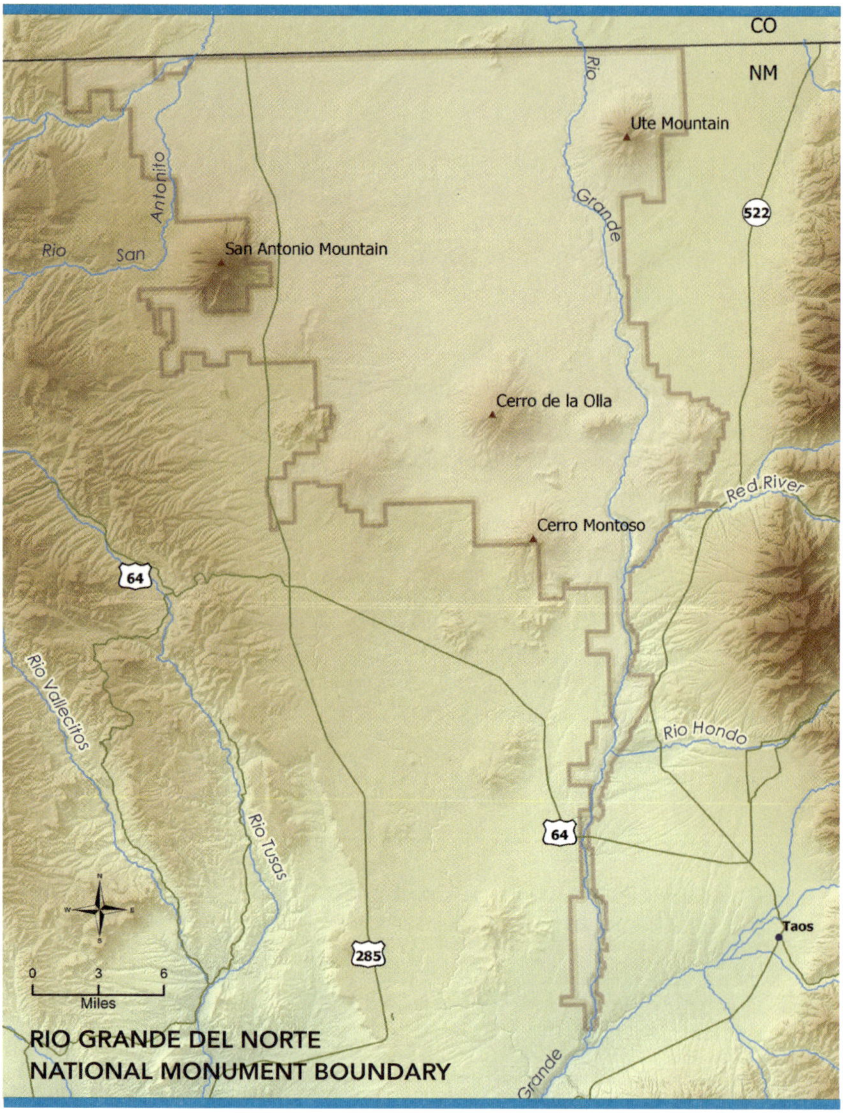

and mayor of the Village of Questa, said the preservation of traditional rights outlined in the Treaty of Guadalupe Hidalgo is an important feature of the new monument. Mayor Garcia attended the White House ceremony for the national monument designation.

"Those of us with deep roots here appreciate that this designation will preserve grazing within the national monument area and specifically protects our right to hunt, fish and collect piñon nuts and firewood," Garcia said. "Monument designation ensures that these ancestral lands will remain for future generations to use and enjoy."

Designation as a national monument was broadly backed by the Taos

County Commission, Taos Village Council, Taos Pueblo, Taos Chamber of Commerce, Taos Green Chamber, Taos Ski Valley, Village of Red River and more than 100 local businesses that recognize the importance monument designation has for local economies.

More Information

The Rio Grande del Norte National Monument is managed by the Bureau of Land Management Taos Field Office:
226 Cruz Alta Road
Taos, NM 87571-5983
575-758-8851
www.blm.gov ❋

Rio Grande del Norte Coalition and Continuing Campaign

BY JOHN OLIVAS

Since the spring of 2008, I have had the pleasure of working on the Rio Grande del Norte campaign. During that time, conservation bills were introduced in the 111th, 112th and 113th Congress. On March 25, 2013, President Barack Obama signed the proclamation to designate and protect 243,555 acres of land mostly owned and managed by the federal Bureau of Land Management office based out of Taos.

During the past five years, a coalition of Taos community members working to protect the area has grown to include elected officials, business owners, the Taos County Chamber of Commerce, the Taos Green Chamber of Commerce, grazing permitees, land grant leaders, acequia parciantes and maroydomos, sportsmen and many local residents. The coalition was recognized by our federal delegation and leadership in Washington, D.C., as a model for protecting public land in the United States.

I am now working on putting a friends group together for the Rio Grande del Norte National Monument. Coalition members, local organizations and Taos citizens are partnering to work on items within the newly designated monument. Partnerships with the Taos Bureau of Land Management will focus on smaller projects and hikes in the area. Meetings are ongoing, so if you're interested in participating in this program, please contact me at *john@nmwild.org* or call 505-379-5551.

NM Wild is continuing to work on wilderness designations within the Rio Grande del Norte National Monument. See the map on Page 17 for more information about the two new wilderness areas we are proposing and subscribe to our eNews via our homepage at *www.nmwild.org* to get the latest information about this and our other campaigns. ❋

Timeline of NM Wild's Involvement in the Rio Grande del Norte Campaign

BUREAU OF LAND MANAGEMENT

May 18, 2010: Rep. Ben Ray Luján introduces legislation for Rio Grande del Norte NCA and Wilderness (co-sponsored by Rep. Martin Heinrich) in the House of Representatives.

August 2010: NM Wild arranges a flyover of the area with media from the *Santa Fe New Mexican*, a freelance writer, a member of NM Wild's Wilderness Outdoor Connection Leadership Program and a Santa Fe County Commissioner. An additional flyover is conducted later that month and includes staff from Rep. Luján and Sens. Bingaman and Udall as well as Taos County elected officials.

2007: NM Wild staff member Jim O'Donnell starts work on the Rio Grande del Norte campaign.

June 2007: Former New Mexico Gov. Bill Richardson signs letter of support for the Rio Grande del Norte National Conservation Area.

2008: NM Wild Traditional Community Organizer John Olivas begins working on the campaign. Olivas quickly gains support of the Northern New Mexico land grant community, which all starts in the living room of Questa Mayor Esther Garcia.

June 2008: Land Grant of San Antonio del Rio Colorado signs a resolution of support.

April 2009: Sen. Bingaman introduces El Rio Grande del Norte National Conservation Area legislation into the 111th Congress (co-sponsored by Sen. Tom Udall).

May 2009: Taos and Mora Valley chambers of commerce sign unanimous resolutions of support for the legislation.

May 2009: Taos County Commission passes resolution in support of the conservation area.

March 2011: Rio Grande del Norte National Conservation Area legislation is re-introduced into the 112th Congress in both the House (H.R. 1241) and Senate (S.667).

March 2012: Faced with a stalled 112th Congress, the coalition switched tracks. Rather than continuing to pursue national monument legislation, the coalition lobbied for designation through executive order under the 1906 Antiquities Act.

May 2012: Taos County Commission passes an updated resolution of support for the Rio Grande del Norte National Monument asking President Barack Obama to utilize his executive powers to designate the area as a protected landscape.

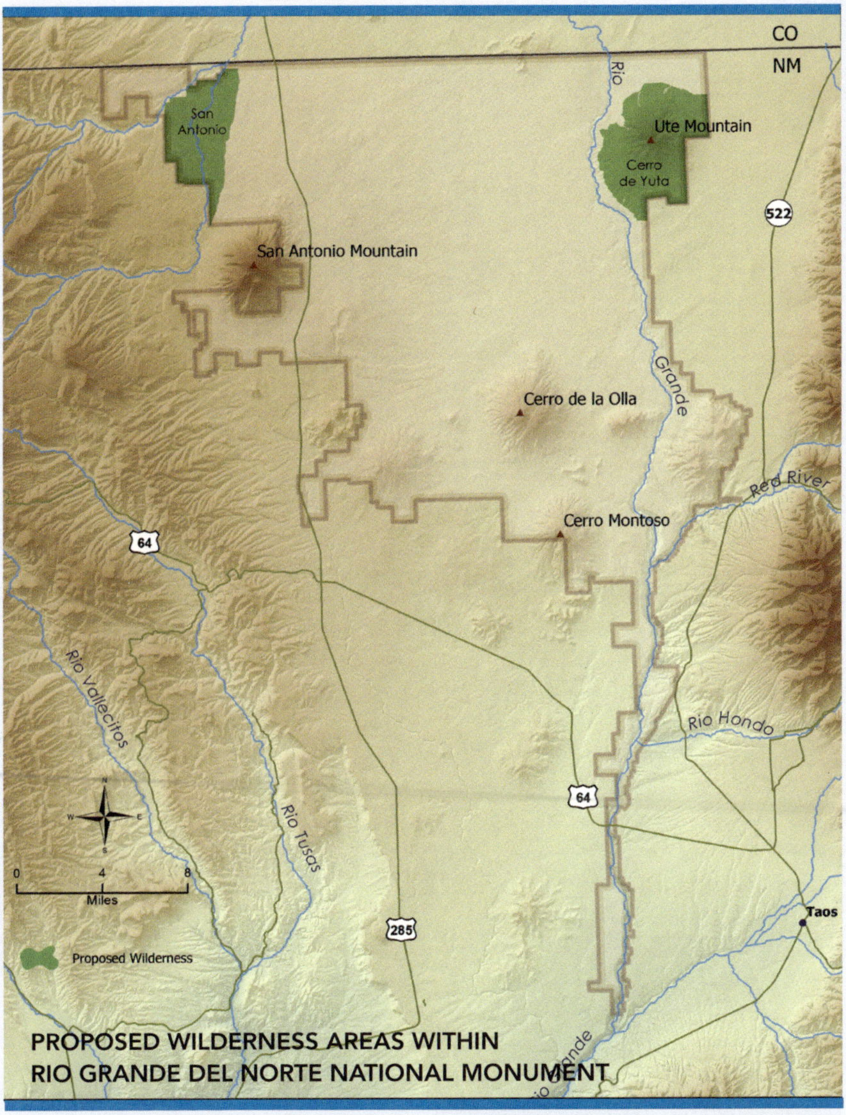

June 2012: Taos County Chamber of Commerce passes an updated resolution of support for the monument.
January 2013: Pueblo of Taos signs resolution of support.
February 2013: Sens. Heinrich and Udall and Rep. Luján reintroduce bills to establish the Río Grande del Norte Conservation Area to protect more than 240,000 acres of BLM-managed lands in Taos and Rio Arriba Counties.
March 25, 2013: President Obama signs declaration creating the new monument.
April 2013-present: NM Wild continues to push for wilderness designation within the national monument boundaries.

ORGAN MOUNTAINS-DESERT PEAKS: Creative Partnerships Define Campaign

BY NATHAN SMALL

On the precipice of permanent protection, the community-supported Organ Mountains-Desert Peaks National Monument and wilderness proposal enjoys exciting momentum because of diverse supporters, creative partnerships and its intersection of natural and cultural landscapes. However, the proposed monument remains threatened by resource destruction, desecration and special interest attempts to delay and dilute permanent protections. This promises to be a momentous year for the national monument effort. Read more to learn about the Organ Mountains-Desert Peaks and visit *www.organmountains.org/take-action* to help permanently protect the area!

Creative partnerships helped define 2013 in the Organ Mountains-Desert Peaks, with the New Mexico Wilderness Alliance (NM Wild) playing a pivotal role each and every time. Doña Ana County youth employed by the Groundworks Green Team (and guided by an NM Wild staffer) surveyed proposed monument lands for cultural resources and discovered more than a dozen important sites; the Las Cruces Green Chamber of Commerce funded an independent economic study showing nearly $7.5 million would flow annually to the area economy from monument designation; and 30 clergy members joined the faith-based group CAFé in calling on President Obama and Sens. Tom Udall and Martin Heinrich to create the Organ Mountains-Desert Peaks National Monument. Local sportsmen formed Sportsmen for the Desert Peaks, showcasing women, youth and families that depend upon the mountains, grasslands and canyons that the monument would protect forever, while business owners and elected officials from Northern New Mexico traveled to Las Cruces to share the benefits of the recently designated Rio Grande del Norte National Monument. Audubon New Mexico completed survey work in the southern Sierra de Las Uvas grasslands, highlighting the area's values as a home for year-round and

Doña Ana Mountains, view to the east

migrating bird species. World War II bombardier Bill Greenberg traveled to Las Cruces from Tucson to revisit, and joined NM Wild to fly over the aerial targets that are part of the proposed monument and which were critical to his training on the Norden bombsight. Ysleta del Sur Pueblo members visited the proposed monument and then traveled to Washington, D.C., to lobby for its permanent protection. At its national conference, the League of United Latin American Citizens (LULAC), passed a resolution

Early Hours Hike

DATE: August 19

DESCRIPTION: Wildlife is always most active in the early hours. Join area experts to learn more mule deer, javelina and desert pronghorn antelope and others—and hopefully see some of them in their native habitats in the Sierra de Las Uvas grasslands.

SEE PAGE 63 FOR DETAILS.

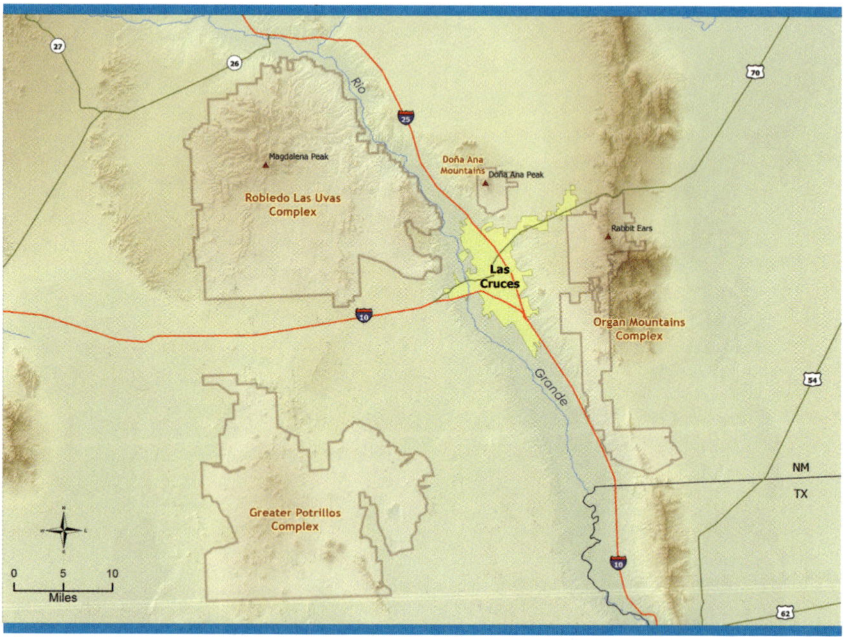

ORGAN MOUNTAINS–DESERT PEAKS NATIONAL MONUMENT

that includes a call for the protection of the Organ Mountains-Desert Peaks.

Like native gramma grass gone to seed, these partnerships have sprung forth from the fertile lands that comprise the proposed monument. They include slightly more than 500,000 acres of Bureau of Land Management (BLM) managed public lands in the largely unprotected Chihuahuan Desert. Astonishingly diverse, elevation levels range from nearly 9,000 feet at the picturesque peaks of the Organ Mountains to 3,900 feet at the bottom of Kilbourne Hole National Natural Landmark. The different habitats and wide elevation range lead to exceptional plant, animal and bird species diversity.

What makes the Organ Mountains-Desert Peaks truly unique is its history and nationally significant cultural heritage. Places like Conklin's Cave in the Organ Mountains and Shelter Cave in the Robledo Mountains have yielded artifacts dating the area's human history back more than 8,000 years. Archaic petroglyphs in areas like Providence Cone and parts of the Sierra de Las Uvas are tantalizing signs of likely habitation sites that, if properly and respectfully studied, could open new windows into the movements of ancient cultures that called these areas home. Emphasizing how deep the cultural legacy runs is the fact that an independent archaeological report completed in 2012 estimated that only 5 percent of the total area included in the proposed national monument has been scientifically studied, a finding that leads experts and novices alike to believe there is far more to learn about this magical region.

This cultural history also includes significant, often tragic chapters from the period known as the Apache Wars that helped define the southwestern frontier all the way through the late 19th century. Massacre Peak, Fillmore Canyon, heliograph sites atop the Robledo Mountains, Slocum's Fort and Lloyd's Ranch all saw significant battles or were traversed by combatants moving from one area to another. Western expansion depended upon the Butterfield Overland Stagecoach trail, currently under consideration for designation as a national historic trail. Named after John W. Butterfield, who partnered with William G. Fargo among others, the Butterfield Stagecoach Trail was America's mail route to the West Coast from 1857 to 1861.

With so many cultural and historical sites, desecration and even large-scale looting are serious concerns. Unchecked off-road vehicle use and industrial development also threaten fragile Chihuahuan Desert wildlands, as well as the plants, animals and recreationists who depend upon those areas. Special interest-led groups have also begun new efforts to try to delay or dilute national monument protections. While rejected by most of the community, including the more than 80 percent of respondents who supported the comprehensive Organ Mountains-Desert Peaks National Monument in a fall 2012 public opinion poll, these special interests found a willing ear with Rep. Steve Pearce, who introduced a shockingly small proposal to protect only parts of the Organ Mountains.

Fortunately, Udall and Heinrich are partnering to introduce comprehensive legislation to protect the Organ Mountains-Desert Peaks. After extensive community input stretching back over six years, the senators' legislation would demonstrate to President Obama and administration officials how much the community wants to protect the Organ Mountains-Desert Peaks. Other legislative benefits include addressing longstanding wilderness study areas and expansion of the popular Trackways National Monument.

There will be more creative partnerships and ever-growing support as the rest of New Mexico learns about the Organ Mountains-Desert Peaks region. Nationally, there is growing recognition that designation of this national monument will protect an ecological area, the Chihuahuan Desert, severely underrepresented in our protected lands system; honor the region's native, Hispanic and multicultural heritage; and bring economic, spiritual and quality of life benefits. Visit *www.organmountains.org* to learn more, find time to visit this enchanting region and help lobby for designation of the Organ Mountains-Desert Peaks National Monument.

For more information go to
www.organmountains.org

Follow Us on Facebook
www.facebook.com/organmountains

COLUMBINE–HONDO:
Essential in Protecting Our Water

BY JOHN OLIVAS, Traditional Community Organizer

LIGHTHAWK

Since 2010, a coalition of citizens and organizations has been working for the permanent protection of one of New Mexico's natural jewels in Northern New Mexico: the Columbine Hondo Wilderness Study Area in Taos County.

Many entities—including the Taos County Commission, Taos Pueblo, Town of Taos, Village of Questa, Village of Red River, Taos Ski Valley and Taos County Chamber of Commerce as well as hundreds of other organizations, businesses and individuals—have formally weighed in to support this area being designated as wilderness in the 113th Congress under the leadership of Sens. Tom Udall and Martin Heinrich and Reps. Ben Ray Luján and Michelle Lujan Grisham. On April 23, 2013, our New Mexico federal delegation reintroduced the Columbine Hondo Wilderness Act, S. 776 and H.R. 1683.

The coalition supporting the campaign is comprised of local wilderness outfitters, livestock permittees, acequia parciantes and mayordomos, hunters, horsemen, fishermen, mountain bikers, and citizens from Taos and the surrounding areas of Taos Ski Valley, Questa, San Cristobal, Valdez, Arroyo Seco, Red River and many other communities.

Community organizations such as the Arroyo Hondo Arriba Community and Rio San Antonio de Colorado Community land grants also are part of the coalition.

Columbine Hondo is situated in a chain of protected areas in the southern Sangre de Cristo Mountains and remains one of the last areas to be protected within this chain.

The Columbine Hondo Wilderness Study Area encompasses 45,000-plus acres in the Sangre de Cristo Mountains. It includes the wild and roadless mountains bounded by the Red River highway on the north side and the Taos Ski Valley on the south end and lies west of the Upper Red River Valley east of the communities of Lama, San Cristobal and Gallina Canyon. Flag Mountain and Lobo Peak are included, as is the study area's highest peak, Gold Hill at 12,703 feet in elevation. The Wheeler Peak Wilderness forms the boundary on the south and east.

The Columbine Hondo Wilderness Study Area has been

> This area is essential in protecting water resources for local acequia members, farmers and many other users along the Rio Grande watershed in New Mexico.

managed essentially as wilderness since it was designated in the New Mexico Wilderness Act back in 1980. Congress formally recognized the wilderness values and characteristics of the Columbine Hondo area and gave it interim protection as a wilderness study area (WSA). In the past 30-plus years, the area has become more deserving of permanent inclusion in the National Wilderness Preservation System, which would ensure that mining, roads, clear cutting and other industrial development would not carve up this special place. The 1964 Wilderness Act allows special areas to be protected for people to enjoy such things as grazing, hiking, camping, hunting and fishing. A slower, more natural pace is emphasized in wilderness areas, which prohibit motorized and mechanized travel.

This area is essential in protecting water resources for local acequia members, farmers and many other users along the Rio Grande watershed in New Mexico. Snows that accumulate in the headwaters area contained within Columbine Hondo melt into streams that drain into the Rio Hondo, Red River and Rio Grande, providing life-giving water for Taos County communities as well as for the central corridor of our desert state. Mayordomos from Lama, San Cristobal, Valdez, Arroyo Hondo and DesMontes divert some of these flowing waters to village acequias that water livestock, orchards and gardens.

Columbine Hondo is situated in a chain of protected areas in the southern Sangre de Cristo Mountains and remains one of the last areas to be protected within this chain. This designation would ensure that this watershed is protected along with areas like Valle Vidal, Latir Wilderness, Wheeler Peak Wilderness, Pecos Wilderness and the Rio Grande del Norte National Monument.

The Columbine Hondo Wilderness Study Area includes rare alpine tundra habitat above 11,000 feet.

Llama Trek in Columbine-Hondo

DATE: August 12

DESCRIPTION: Wild Earth Llama Adventures is partnering with the NM Wild on a llama trip into the Columbine Hondo Wilderness Study Area. This day hike is a great way to experience the unspoiled wilderness near Taos. Llamas will carry your gear while naturalist guides share their knowledge of southern Rocky Mountain ecology. Enjoy a sumptuous feast prepared by the guides in a pristine wilderness setting.

SEE PAGE 60 FOR DETAILS.

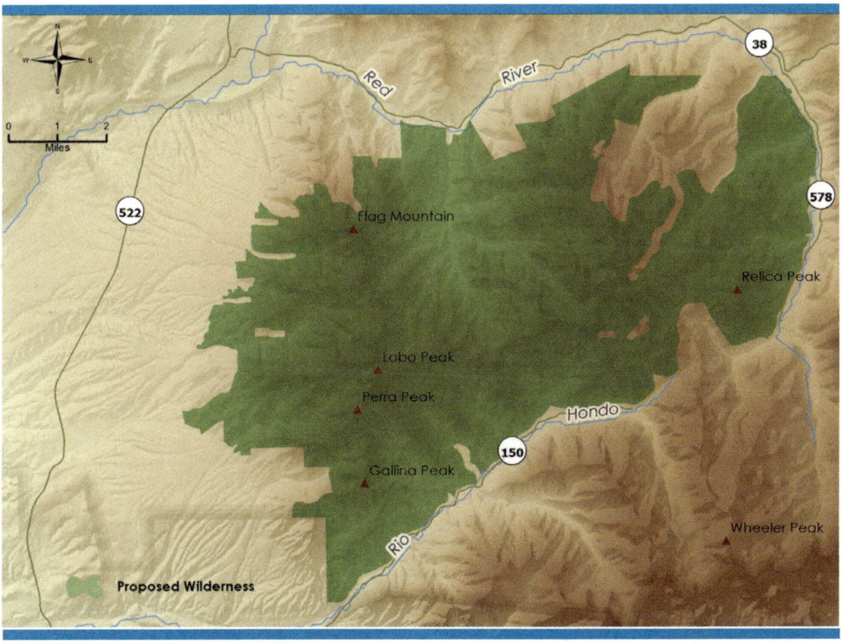

PROPOSED COLUMBINE-HONDO WILDERNESS

It is crowned by 13 miles of high alpine ridges and peaks that tower. The Columbine Hondo area is a refuge for many species of wildlife, and human visitors might see elk, mountain lion, deer, black bear, Rocky Mountain bighorn sheep, Rio Grande cutthroat trout, pika, marmot, pine marten or birds of prey. These mountains are an important wildlife migratory corridor between the Latir Peak and Wheeler Peak wilderness areas.

The next step is designation as permanent wilderness, the highest form of protection and a ban on all development. Former Sen. Jeff Bingaman introduced legislation to protect Columbine-Hondo in the 112th Congress, but it stalled along with dozens of other conservation bills. The Columbine Hondo Wilderness Coalition is hopeful that Congress chooses to lead this year and protect New Mexico's wilderness study area.

Please join the efforts to protect the Columbine Hondo Wilderness Study Area. Contact the New Mexico Wilderness Alliance for additional details.

For more information go to **http://www.columbinehondo.org**

Follow Us on Facebook **www.facebook.com/ColumbineHondoWilderness**

OTERO MESA: Protecting Desert Grasslands

BY JUDY CALMAN

Otero Mesa is one of the most special places in New Mexico. It is the largest remaining unfragmented Chihuahuan Desert grassland in the United States, has tens of thousands of ancient petroglyphs and archaeological sites, and has a genetically pure, native herd of pronghorn. It also sits on one of the largest untapped aquifers in the state.

Our campaign to protect Otero Mesa has been ongoing since 2001, when the New Mexico Wilderness Alliance (NM Wild) helped form the Coalition for Otero Mesa, a broad coalition of hunters, ranchers, conservationists and state leaders. The coalition has led the way in preserving this last great desert grassland and protecting the landscape from threats of oil and gas drilling and hard rock mining.

Otero Mesa had its share of excitement in the past year. The Bureau of Land Management's (BLM) Draft Resource Management Plan (RMP), governing Otero, Sierra and Doña Ana counties was issued in April 2013. Among other things, the plan proposed a fairly large Area of Critical Environmental Concern (ACEC) for Otero Mesa, totaling almost 200,000 acres. We've been working very hard on the RMP, urging the BLM to propose an even larger ACEC for the grasslands and to ensure through stronger management that the amazing values in the area are truly well protected.

We've also been insisting that the

NATHAN NEWCOMER

BLM complete an inventory of Otero Mesa for areas with wilderness characteristics, something it is required to do during the RMP process but did not successfully finish.

Another major issue facing Otero Mesa is the BLM's recent drive to lease parcels in Otero County for oil and gas development for the first time in more than 15 years. Until now, the Las Cruces BLM has not leased in this area because it lacked a valid (and required) oil and gas leasing plan—something that should have been addressed in the RMP, but which is being delayed for several years by the BLM, leaving the office without the authority to lease until a plan is finalized. While not directly inside the grasslands, any leasing inside the county without a legitimate oil and gas leasing plan is a serious threat to Otero Mesa and is not supported by current law and agency guidance.

We are working hard to ensure there is no leasing in any part of Otero County until the BLM completes a solid environmental analysis of potential impacts from development and excludes sensitive areas like the grasslands from leasing entirely.

For more information go to
www.oteromesa.org

Follow Us on Facebook
facebook.com/nmwilderness

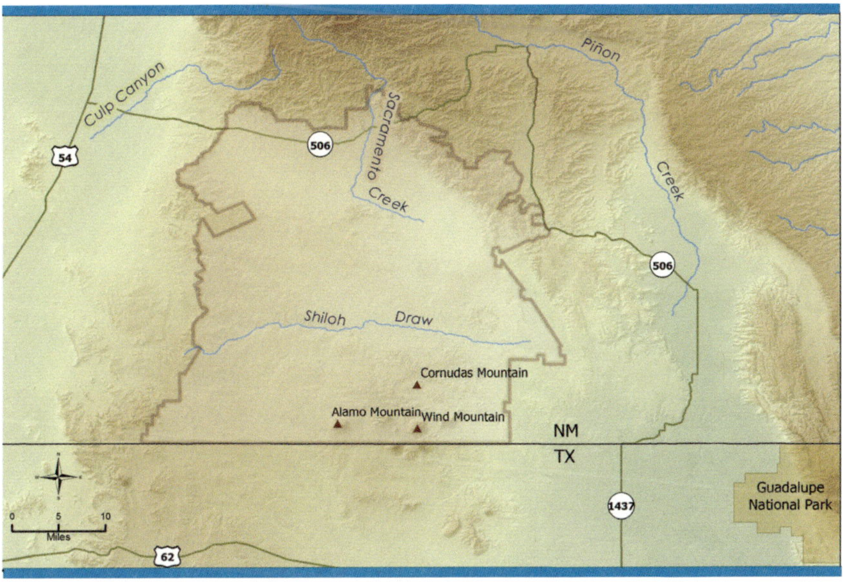

OTERO MESA CAMPAIGN

Otero Mesa is one of the most special places in New Mexico. It is the largest remaining unfragmented Chihuahuan Desert grassland in the United States.

Dawn on Otero Mesa; Great Horned Owl; petroglyphs on Alamo Mountain

DAWN & OWL: PAULA EASTWOOD; PETROGLYPHS: NATHAN NEWCOMER

MEXICAN GRAY WOLF/GILA WILDERNESS:

Strides Made for Gila and Wolves

STAFF REPORT

Fifteen years after they were reintroduced, fewer than 75 Mexican gray wolves remain in the wild in New Mexico and Arizona.

Mexican gray wolves are not only a majestic living symbol of the Southwest, but they're also a critically important top predator. Mexican gray wolves and the reintroduction program continue to face serious threats, and that's why the New Mexico Wilderness Alliance remains persistent in its work to ensure the successful return of the lobo.

Thanks to the support of those who share an interest in creating a safe home for our state's native wolves, NM Wild has been able to take several positive steps to protect the Mexican gray wolf in the past year.

In 2013, we celebrated the 15th anniversary of the reintroduction of the Mexican gray wolf to the Southwest with a variety of events across the state including a "Happy Birthday Lobos" event in Silver City. In October, we joined several other organizations for a wolf rally in Albuquerque.

With WildEarth Guardians as our partner, we filed a lawsuit against the Department of Justice (DOJ) for its failure to prosecute poachers of wolves in conformance with the Endangered Species Act.

Despite 50 Mexican wolves being illegally shot since their reintroduction to the Southwest in 1998, the DOJ has only prosecuted two

Gila Wolf Backpack

DATE: August 29–September 1

DESCRIPTION: A premium backpack trip looking for wild Mexican wolves in the Gila Wilderness, led by our expert wolf guide, Dave Parsons.This is a unique opportunity to spend time with a wilderness hero in a place he knows and loves like no other. We will be looking for wolves and other wildlife while enjoying the natural beauty of one of the most spectacular wild places in the US. Gila Backcountry Services will be providing all of our meals and pack mules to haul all of our gear.

SEE PAGE 44–45 FOR DETAILS.

individuals. This is due to the DOJ's McKittrick Policy, which states the department will only prosecute if they can prove an individual knew exactly what species he or she was killing. Since the implementation of this policy, poachers have learned to claim they thought they were shooting a coyote when confronted by law enforcement. We will know more about the progress of our lawsuit in the coming months. ❁

WIKIMEDIA COMMONS

Gila Wilderness Update

BY NATHAN NEWCOMER

In the last year, the New Mexico Wilderness Alliance (NM Wild) began preparing for the upcoming Gila National Forest land-use plan revision process. The U.S. Forest Service is slated to begin the process of updating its current land-use plan in the fall. As a part of this effort, we have already begun conducting extensive fieldwork throughout the Gila National Forest, documenting wilderness characteristics and collecting significant scientific data. With close to 2 million acres of public land that need to be inventoried, NM Wild is looking for volunteers in the region to help gather information on the ground. We have planned several workshops throughout the area to train volunteers on how to conduct fieldwork, as well as how to use electronic tablets that will record the data.

We also have held several meetings with the Forest Service to discuss ways that we can work together on community projects that benefit the three wilderness areas in the

NATHAN NEWCOMER

Gila National Forest, as well as the numerous other roadless areas that exist. We already have four projects scheduled that include closing illegal roads that intrude on the existing wilderness areas, citizen monitoring and removal of invasive species. As NM Wild's Gila grassroots organizer, I was invited to give a presentation to the Forest Service's leadership team at the Ladder Ranch in late August 2013. All of the top-level staff from the Gila district attended the meeting and joined discussions about the upcoming 50th anniversary of the Wilderness Act, the National Wilderness Conference to be held in Albuquerque in October and projects that we will partner on together over the next year.

We also continue to coordinate our efforts with sportsmen's organizations advocating Mexican wolf recovery, travel management planning and responsible off-road vehicle use. NM Wild is working with the Upper Gila Watershed Alliance (UGWA), the Gila Resources Information Project (GRIP), the Sierra Club and concerned citizens to support projects that will ensure a long-term water supply for our rural communities by keeping the Gila River—the lifeblood of the region—wild and free

For more information go to
http://www.nmwild.org/our-work/

Follow Us on Facebook
facebook.com/nmwilderness

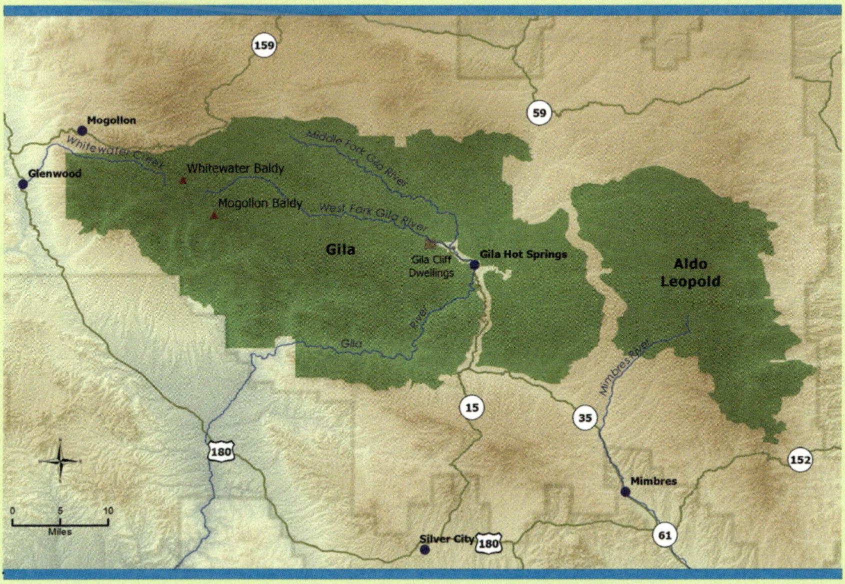

GILA AND ALDO LEOPOLD WILDERNESS

CHACO CANYON:
Continued Threats

STAFF REPORT

Chaco Culture National Historic Park, a major center of ceremony and trade for the prehistoric Four Corners areas, is one of the most spectacular places in New Mexico. This is where the ancient Puebloan culture took root and flourished for more than 300 years. Chaco was at one time the ceremonial, administrative and economic center of the San Juan Basin.

Chaco is famous for its massive stone buildings constructed by the Chacoan people. These "great houses" were multiple stories tall and contained hundreds of rooms. Today guests from all over the world come to enjoy visiting great houses such as Pueblo Bonito and Peñasco Blanco and to receive a small glimpse into Chacoan life. Chaco's combination of natural beauty and cultural significance justifies its World Heritage Site status. However, development continues to threaten Chaco.

Oil and gas drilling on state lands within view of the park's visitor center continues to be a significant threat. In addition, development threatens Chacoan ruins to the north on Bureau of Land Management (BLM) lands. These lands are part of a connective corridor to the Bisti/De-Na-Zin Wilderness through the Ah-Shi-Sle-Pah Wilderness Study Area. It is also clear that oil field dust, air pollutants and noise will reduce visibility while also threatening the health of people and wildlife living downwind from the development.

As such, the New Mexico Wilderness Alliance (NM Wild) supports the creation of approximately 20,000 acres of wilderness within the park to protect this sacred site. We also support protection of BLM lands surrounding the park in order to provide a buffer around the park and its scenic views. In addition, we support a revision of the boundary of the Pueblo Pintado Outlier to include the large ruin and other significant sites.

NM Wild is continuing to participate in the BLM's land use planning decisions for the area around Chaco. In August 2013, the Farmington Field Office of the BLM announced it would allow approximately 30 parcels in the immediate vicinity of the park to be leased for oil and gas development. Fortunately, after a round of comments and outcry from the environmental and Native American communities, the BLM decided to take those parcels off the leasing table for the foreseeable future.

In addition, we intend to be involved at every step as the Farmington office develops an amendment to its Resource Management Plan to complete an inventory of lands with wilderness characteristics and to analyze possible plans for the BLM lands in the Chaco "buffer" zone. We will update our members with progress reports and opportunities for involvement.

DREAMSTIME.COM

Kin Bineola ruins, Chaco Canyon

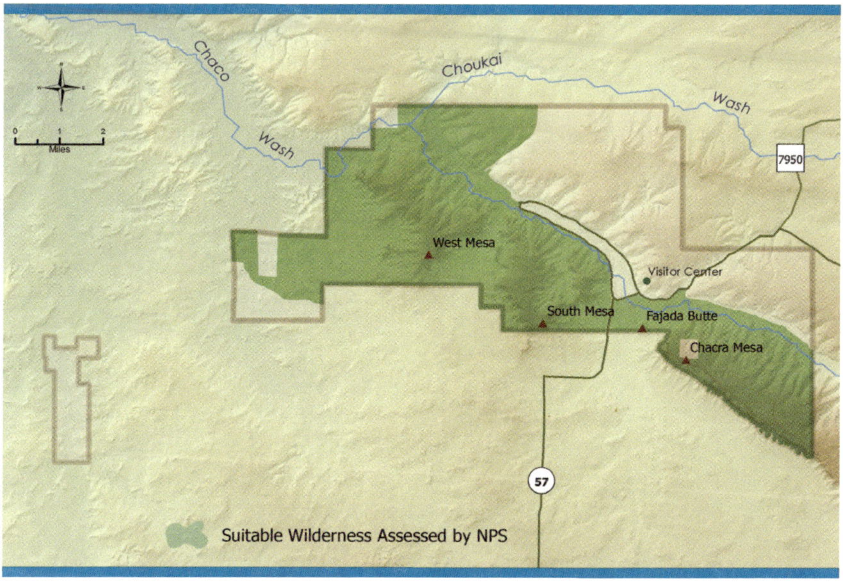

CHACO CULTURE NATIONAL HISTORICAL PARK

LEGAL UPDATE

BY JUDY CALMAN

2013 WAS AN EXCITING LEGAL YEAR FOR THE NEW MEXICO WILDERNESS ALLIANCE!

We filed a lawsuit in May, with WildEarth Guardians as our partner, against the U.S. Department of Justice for its failure to prosecute poachers of wolves in conformance with the Endangered Species Act. The act requires prosecution of people who knowingly harm or kill a species that is listed as threatened or endangered. Despite 50 Mexican wolves being listed by the Fish and Wildlife Service as "illegally shot" since their reintroduction to the Southwest in 1998, the Justice Department has only prosecuted two individuals.

This is due to an internal policy created by the Justice Department called the McKittrick Policy (so named after the case that led to it). The McKittrick Policy, formulated in 1998 without public announcement or comment and without consultation with the Fish and Wildlife Service, requires the department to prove an individual knew exactly what species he or she was harming before prosecution can take place.

This policy is in direct conflict with the Endangered Species Act itself, which does not require such knowledge, and with over 25 years of case law in which courts have confirmed knowledge of the exact endangered species is not required for prosecution.

Not surprisingly, this policy has led to a newfound inability among some members of the public to distinguish between Mexican wolves, coyotes and dogs. Nearly every time someone is questioned about a Mexican wolf death, he or she reports that they thought the animal was a coyote or dog. The result is that the individual is not prosecuted for the crime.

This policy extends to all endangered species, and has been used by the Justice Department to excuse prosecution in shootings of wolves, grizzly bears, condors, Florida panthers, whooping cranes and other treasures of the American landscape. We hope that as our lawsuit progresses, we can put an end to this shocking policy and have a positive impact on Mexican wolves and other endangered species around the country.

We also recently joined a New Mexico Environmental Law Center appeal of the recent "pit rule" revi-

We hope that as our lawsuit progresses, we can have a positive impact on Mexican wolves and other endangered species around the country.

sion by the state's Oil Conservation Commission. In 2012, we participated in the commission's Santa Fe hearings. These hearings were the result of petitions brought by the oil and gas industry shortly after the election of Gov. Susana Martinez and were designed to gut and weaken rules put in place by the Richardson administration, which were protective of groundwater at oil and gas sites.

With the makeup of the commission altered by the change in administration, the commission ruled in favor of the industry's petition, even though none of the evidence has changed since the Richardson-era hearings. As a result, the regulations surrounding the toxic wastewater disposal pits associated with fluid mineral extraction have been severely degraded. Pits can now be located closer to schools, homes and wetlands. Pits can be dug closer to shallow groundwater and can have higher levels of toxins. More "self-regulation" responsibility has been given to the industry, while actual regulatory authority has been taken away from the state. These rules affect every well drilled in New Mexico, whether on state or federal land. We believe these rules will endanger many communities around the state, as well as increase risks to our groundwater, wetlands and wildlife. We have joined the appeal of this rule to the courts and will keep our membership posted as we move forward over the coming year.

We are continuing our oversight of oil and gas extraction, with particular emphasis on Otero Mesa and Chaco Canyon. We are monitoring federal lease sales in those areas, commenting on associated environmental assessments and filing formal protests for parcels we believe should not be leased at all. This year we have taken the additional step of appealing one Bureau of Land Management (BLM) decision to the Washington, D.C.-based Interior Board of Land Appeals. This decision involved the leasing of land in Otero County without a valid management plan to support leasing. We believe the BLM could jeopardize fragile portions of Otero Mesa if they are allowed to continue leasing in Otero County without a management plan.

The Farmington BLM office took the proactive step of pulling many proposed leases around Chaco Canyon out of the leasing pool for the foreseeable future. While this is most welcome news, we will continue to monitor proposed leases in the area and participate in the process where appropriate.

Finally, we continue to monitor the proposed actions of federal agencies to ensure they are compliant with applicable environmental laws and that they are not threatening to the wilderness areas, wilderness study areas and wildlife we all hold so dear. We have developed excellent working relationships with most BLM, Forest Service and Fish and Wildlife Service offices around the state and maintain healthy conversations with them in addition to our formal comments.

Look for additional legal updates in our weekly eNews and always feel free to contact me with any questions or concerns at *judy@nmwild.org*!

“The world is big and I want to have a good look at it before it gets dark.”

—John Muir

Pecos Wilderness

NATHAN NEWCOMER

Hikes, Projects & Special Trips

TO REGISTER FOR ANY EVENT GO TO www.nmwild.org

HIKE REGISTRATION FEES (except special trips and where indicated in description):
$10 for members
$20 for non-members

Yellowstone Winter Wildlife Watch

DATE: February 23–27

PLACE: Mammoth Hot Springs Hotel in Yellowstone National Park and Chico Hot Springs Resort

DESCRIPTION: Join the New Mexico Wilderness Alliance's new Executive Director Mark Allison and special guest David Parsons for three days and four nights in the stunning setting of Yellowstone National Park for our most unique wilderness and wildlife watching experience. We will spend the first days viewing the famous wolves of Lamar Valley—a spectacular opportunity for dramatic photography. We will leave Mammoth Lodge each day at first light to look for wolf packs as they hunt for prey in full view from the roadsides. February is also the ideal time to view elk, bighorn sheep, bison, otters, coyotes and raptors in the beauty of their winter range. After a hearty lunch, the group will enjoy an afternoon snowshoe on the groomed trails of the Northern Range—another excellent opportunity to photograph the unique winter landscape. On the third day, our expert guides will take us out for a day of snowshoeing while providing expert interpretation of the natural history of Yellowstone. We will also meet with wolf reintroduction biologists in the park and visit a renowned photographer—all while enjoying great food, wine and deluxe eco-lodging at the Mammoth lodge. The trip will end at the Chico Hot Springs Resort where we will soak in the historic mineral pools surrounded by Paradise Valley. A dinner at Chico's restaurant, recognized for bringing fine dining to the region, will be a memorable finish to an epic week in the wild! On the morning of February 27, we will enjoy a hearty breakfast in the Chico Lodge and then take a morning soak in the hot springs. Guests depart as necessary that day to meet their flights in Bozeman.

MEALS: All meals are included for three days and four nights. Delicious breakfasts and dinners are provided as part of the package at the historic Mammoth hotel and the gourmet restaurant at Chico Hot Springs. Picnic-style lunches and an abundance of healthy snacks and hot drinks will be provided during the day.

MAXIMUM PARTICIPANTS: 10

TRIP LEADERS: Mark Allison along with special guest David Parsons, carnivore conservation biologist and former Mexican wolf recovery coordinator at the U.S. Fish and Wildlife Service.

PARTICIPANT REQUIREMENTS: Guests must be 18 years or older or 15 years and older accompanied by an adult. All levels of snowshoe ability from beginner to expert are welcome. Guests must be in good physical condition and able to snowshoe on moderate groomed trails at least five miles roundtrip without over-exertion.

TRAVEL ARRANGEMENTS: Transportation will be provided within the park. Guests must provide their own roundtrip transportation to Mammoth Hot Springs Hotel. Airline reservations may be made to the closest airport at Bozeman, Mont., and a car rental or shuttle may be obtained there.

TO SIGN UP: Contact trip leader Mark Allison at *mark@nmwild.org* or 505-239-0906, or sign up online. A $500 deposit is due at time of registration with the balance due on Feb. 10.

COST: $2,500 for members and $2,800 for non-members based on double occupancy. Add $500 for single occupancy. Airfare to Bozeman and transportation to the park are not included. Snowshoes and poles will be provided.

LEFT: NPS/YELLOWSTONE/BARRY O'NEILL; RIGHT: DEMIS FOSTER

PROJECTS & HIKES

Rio Chama Rafting Trip

DATE: June 7-9

DESCRIPTION: Experience three days and two nights floating down America's wild and scenic Rio Chama with experts, scientists and philosophers from the New Mexico Wilderness Alliance (NM Wild). The 25-mile long Rio Chama begins in alpine woodlands as a clear, rushing trout stream and ends at the head of Abiquiu Reservoir as a silty, desert river, rolling among rainbow cliffs typical of the Four Corners region. Lovely, wooded campsites and lively, but easy rapids make the Chama one of the best family river outings anywhere.

MAXIMUM PARTICIPANTS: 12

MEALS: Gourmet food and beverages will be provided.

TRIP LEADER: Doug Chinn

PARTICIPANT REQUIREMENTS: First-time rafters are welcome. Participants must be 12 or older and in normal good health. Guides will do the navigating in our oar-powered, self-bailing rafts. You also can choose to use an individual inflatable kayak on this Class II river.

DRIVING TIME: One hour north of Santa Fe, two hours north of Albuquerque.

CONTACT: 505-948-1154 or *dougbike@comcast.net*

COST: A $500 deposit is required at the time of signup. **Trip cost is $1,000 for NM Wild members and $1,200 for non-members** (includes gourmet food and beverages for three days and two nights, equipment, shuttle to the river from meeting place in Abiquiu and river instruction).

Dinosaur tracks on the banks of the Rio Chama

DEMIS FOSTER

ABOVE & RIGHT: PAULA EASTWOOD

Gila Wolf Backpack

SPECIAL PREMIUM TRIP

NATHAN NEWCOMER

DATE: August 29 – September 1

DESCRIPTION: A four-day, three-night luxury backpack trip looking for wild Mexican wolves in the Gila Wilderness. Our expert guide, Dave Parsons, led the wolf reintroduction project for the U.S. Fish and Wildlife Service in the '90s. No one knows more about Mexican wolves or has done more for them than Parsons. This is a truly unique opportunity to spend time with a wilderness hero in a place he knows and loves like no other. We will be looking for wolves and other wildlife while enjoying the natural beauty of one of the most spectacular wild places in the lower 48 states. Zack Crockett with Gila Backcountry Services (www.gilabackcountryservices.com) will be providing pack mules to haul most of our gear in, and he will also be providing all of our meals.

MAXIMUM PARTICIPANTS: 12

TRIP LEADER: Dave Parsons

HIKING DISTANCE: 4.5 miles to base camp and another 20-plus miles (optional) on day hikes exploring the wilderness.

LOCATION: The Gila Wilderness is in southwest New Mexico, five hours south of Albuquerque.

COST: $800, including all meals and transport of gear.

NOTE: For this exclusive trip, mules will transport your backpack gear to base camp so you can enjoy hiking with only a daypack. We will camp near water, so you will only need enough water for the hike in. Tents and sleeping bags can be provided for an additional $50 per person.

JAMES BROSKA

PROJECTS & HIKES

The Importance of Service Projects

BY ROXANNE PACHECO

One of my favorite places to camp, hike and get away from the hot city is the beautiful Jemez Mountains. So when the opportunity to participate in a service project cleaning up illegal camp sites along the Jemez River Canyon arose I didn't hesitate to volunteer. I asked my grandson Manny and my nephew Isaac if they wanted to join me as they often do on my hiking and camping adventures; they didn't hesitate either.

So on a bright summer day we headed out to Jemez. Of course, we stopped at the pueblo for some scrumptious hot fry bread, sat in the shade of the red rock walls and took in the surroundings while munching on our snack. The plan was to meet our fellow volunteers at the Jemez Falls Campground, get a good night's sleep and head out on the trail early the next morning to meet the forest ranger and see what she had planned for us.

After a hot meal of breakfast burritos, we headed out to the trail and met the ranger. She had tons of garbage bags, canvas bags and grates (we used these to sift through and take out the old burned wood from the fire pits). She explained that people camped on the river illegally and left behind their trash and fire rings, which were affecting the riparian surroundings. So the plan was to hike in a ways with our tools and then work our way back with our bags full of trash and charred remains from the campfire debris and to keep repeating the process until we had made an impact on the trail.

Among the volunteers was a couple who had been vacationing in Santa Fe with their teenage daughter and her friend. They had come across the Wild Guide, saw the project and decided to help out. They said they tried to find volunteer projects when vacationing. We all got right to work picking up the trash, sifting the charred campfire debris into the canvas bags, hauling it all back to the trailhead and putting it in the Forest Service trucks. We picked up hundreds of dirty socks, tons of dirty diapers and hundreds of empty Bud Light cans. We took apart dozens of fire rings, spread the rocks, cleaned up the debris and hauled it all out. The forest ranger was so appreciative because this area had not been cleaned up in years and we made a huge difference. I was so proud of my boys—they worked so hard and were so proud of the difference we made.

Service projects are one of the most important things we do here at the New Mexico Wilderness Alliance. Not only do you get the satisfaction of making a difference but you meet great people, see beautiful places and connect with our Mother Earth.

I encourage everyone to try to get out and help with a service project this year. Hopefully, I will see you on the trail in 2014.

BLUE RANGE WILDERNESS VOLUNTEER SERVICE PROJECT 1

Wilderness Boundary Signage & Road Closures

VOLUNTEER SERVICE PROJECT

DATE: February 21-23

DESCRIPTION: Often dubbed New Mexico's forgotten wilderness, the Blue Range Wilderness is nestled on the border with Arizona, and the Gila Wilderness is just a stone's throw away to the east. Located in the heart of the Blue Range Wolf Recovery Area, the region is the only place left in the United States where the endangered Mexican gray wolf is actively being reintroduced into the wild.

Working with the Gila National Forest, we will overhaul signage along the wilderness boundary, as well as construct barriers to prevent illegal ATV intrusion into the wilderness. We will basecamp at Kelly Campground and work along the eastern and southern boundary of the wilderness.

MAXIMUM PARTICIPANTS: 15

HIKE LEADER: Nathan Newcomer, Gila grassroots organizer

HIKING DISTANCE: 6 miles

CONTACT: *nathan@nmwild.org*

NATHAN NEWCOMER

BEACON IN THE DESERT: Providence Cone Human History Tour

GUIDED HIKE

DATE: February 22

DESCRIPTION: Providence Cone rises more than 300 feet from the surrounding Chihuahuan Desert scrubland. Long a beacon for native peoples who traveled near and far, the cultural importance of Providence Cone is only now becoming known. After late summer monsoons, area flowers explode and a wide variety of wildlife use the area, including our scaled friends who lend it another name, “Rattlesnake Rock.” On our February tour we will explore a mesmerizing human history through the expert eyes of local interpreters and come to understand why Providence Cone is a very apt name for this uniquely positioned cultural touchstone.

MAXIMUM PARTICIPANTS: 15

HIKE LEADER: Angel Peña

HIKING DISTANCE: 1.5 miles (plus optional scramble up and around Providence Cone)

CONTACT: *angeldigs@gmail.com*

WIKIMEDIA COMMONS

WORKSHOP PHOTOS: MICHAEL GRADY

MAP & COMPASS COURSE WITH MICHAEL GRADY Ojito Wilderness

DATE: March 20 and 22

Classroom Session
7-9 p.m., Thursday, March 20
New Mexico Wilderness Alliance Albuquerque Office

Field Session
6-8 mile cross country hike in the Ojito Wilderness
8 a.m. to 5 p.m., Saturday, March 22
Carpool from NM Wild Albuquerque office, round trip 100 miles.

DESCRIPTION: Learn map and compass navigation from one of the best. Michael Grady has hiked off-trail in New Mexico, using only map and compass, since 1984. He is a past president of the New Mexico Mountain Club and teaches Map & Compass for the Mountain Club and for UNM Continuing Education.

Participants must be able and willing to hike cross country in rough terrain for at least six miles. Bring your own food, rain gear, sunscreen, pack with a minimum of three liters of water, good hiking boots that are not new, and a base-plate compass with adjustable declination. Maps will be provided.

MAXIMUM PARTICIPANTS: 8

COST: $40

CONTACT: Lynne Uhring, *lynne@nmwild.org* or 505-843-8696, ext. 110

Kilbourne Hole panorama

BLUE RANGE WILDERNESS VOLUNTEER SERVICE PROJECT 2

Invasive Plant Removal

VOLUNTEER SERVICE PROJECT

DATE: March 21–23

DESCRIPTION: Often dubbed New Mexico's forgotten wilderness, the Blue Range Wilderness is nestled on the border with Arizona, and the Gila Wilderness is just a stone's throw away to the east. Located in the heart of the Blue Range Wolf Recovery Area, the region is the only place left in the United States where the endangered Mexican gray wolf is actively being reintroduced into the wild.

Working with the Gila National Forest, we will conduct citizen-based surveys and the removal of invasive, noxious weeds that have begun to encroach on the Blue Range Wilderness. We will basecamp at Pueblo Park and spend our days hiking in the canyons of the Blue Range, as well as Aspen Mountain.

MAXIMUM PARTICIPANTS: 30

HIKE LEADER: Nathan Newcomer, Gila grassroots organizer

HIKING DISTANCE: 6–8 miles

CONTACT: *nathan@nmwild.org*

TOP: WIKIMEDIA COMMONS; RIGHT: NASA

RIM CLEANUP
Kilbourne Hole

DATE: March 29

DESCRIPTION: Kilbourne Hole volcanic crater is a National Natural Landmark about 25 miles southwest of Las Cruces. The crater has helped astronauts train for the Apollo Space Program and is a popular recreational area. Unfortunately, trash has accumulated around parking areas, degrading the area and dishonoring the incredible scientific, natural and historical values of this incredible gem. So, join the New Mexico Wilderness Alliance and other local organizations in helping to clean up Kilbourne Hole rim!

MAXIMUM PARTICIPANTS: 40

PROJECT LEADERS: Angel Peña and Nathan Small

CONTACT: *nathan.p.small@gmail.com, angeldigs@gmail.com*

Apollo 17 Command Module

Sierra de las Uvas Mountains

JEFF STEINBORN

VOLUNTEER SERVICE PROJECT

Sierra de las Uvas
Grassland Restoration Exploration

DATE: April 12

DESCRIPTION: The Sierra de Las Uvas Mountains are filled with cultural, ecological and scenic treasures. But some lands to the east are severely degraded with overwhelming shrub invasion and loss of plant and wildlife diversity. Join us as we survey the healthy part of the Sierra de Las Uvas to prevent such a fate from invading these iconic mountains. We also will plan ways to build up good soils and prevent erosion, using cutting-edge watershed restoration techniques. This will be a multi-year effort, but good on the ground reconnaissance is an essential first step to success. Help us start on the right foot!

MAXIMUM PARTICIPANTS: 20

PROJECT LEADERS: Angel Peña and Nathan Small

CONTACT:
nathan.p.small@gmail.com
angeldigs@gmail.com

Urban Reach Rio Grande Float Trip

DATE: May 3

DESCRIPTION: Join the New Mexico Wilderness Alliance (NM Wild) and Far Flung Adventures to explore the primitive aspects of the lifeline of New Mexico from Algodones to the Alameda Bridge (water level permitting). Our experienced guides and conservationists will provide history and discuss important issues about this highly managed, but gorgeous stretch of the Rio Grande River.

MAXIMUM PARTICIPANTS: 25

COST: **$75, including river rafts or inflatable kayaks, gear, guides, lunch and shuttle.**

TRIP TIME: 5- to 6-hour tour

TRIP LEADERS: **Steve Harris** is the owner of Far Flung Adventures and executive director of Rio Grande Restoration, which works with water and natural resources management agencies and individual stakeholders to develop policies and programs that will protect the Rio Grande and its tributaries from the ecological impacts of over-diversion.

Todd Schulke is a co-founder and senior staff member for the Center for Biological Diversity. He has been involved in forest and river protection and restoration in the Southwest for more than 20 years. Schulke is an experienced river runner and has been on the board of directors of NM Wild since its inception.

CONTACT: tisha@nmwild.org

JOE ALCOCK

May Wildflower Exploration

DATE: May 4

DESCRIPTION: If winter rains combine with spring showers, the Organ Mountains-Desert Peaks area comes alive in a sea of wildflowers. Depending on where the flowers are brightest, we might travel to the secluded grasslands of the Sierra de Las Uvas Mountains, the verdant foothills of the Organ Mountains, the remote and lush mountain grasslands in the Potrillo Mountains or the hidden lava canyons in the lava flows. These landscapes are some of the most important bird, animal and plant habitat anywhere in southern New Mexico, and you'll be our guest as we see them in what is hopefully full bloom!

HIKE LEADER: Angel Peña.

HIKING DISTANCE: Up to 5 miles

CONTACT: *angeldigs@gmail.com*

GUIDED HIKE

BUREAU OF LAND MANAGEMENT

Lower San Francisco Canyon

BUREAU OF LAND MANAGEMENT

DATE: May 10

DESCRIPTION: Riverine habitat and wetlands make up less than 1 percent of New Mexico's landscape, and we will explore some of the finest remaining river country in the state. This somewhat strenuous hike will take us to the Lower San Francisco River where it winds its way through a critical wilderness study area. With its towering cliff walls, hot springs, ancient narrow-leaf and Fremont cottonwoods, native walnut and giant Arizona sycamore trees, this river corridor is home to a remarkable diversity of birds, fish and mammals. Seldom visited, the Lower San Francisco Canyon will surely provide outstanding opportunities for solitude and unconfined forms of recreation. Be sure to bring your "river legs!"

MAXIMUM PARTICIPANTS: 10

HIKE LEADER: Nathan Newcomer, Gila grassroots organizer

HIKING DISTANCE: 6 miles

CONTACT: *nathan@nmwild.org*

Rio Grande Del Norte Rafting Trip

SPECIAL DAY TRIP

DATE: May 31

DESCRIPTION: Los Rios River Runners is partnering with the New Mexico Wilderness Alliance for a river raft trip through the recently designated Rio Grande del Norte National Monument.

Spend a full day on the river in the spectacular Rio Grande Gorge with walls rising to 1,500 feet. We will spend the morning in the gentle Orilla Verde section, flanked by green meadows. It's mellow and peaceful, the perfect introduction to the gorgeous Rio Grande Gorge. After a riverside lunch, we head into the rollercoaster Class III rapids of the Racecourse.

This will be an excellent trip for those who want to experience the thrill of whitewater, but ease gradually into it. After a morning getting comfortable with the paddle in your hand, you'll feel ready to tackle the Narrows, Eye of the Needle, Sleeping Beauty and the finishing thrill of Souse Hole. This trip is not recommended for children 12 and under during high water conditions.

MAXIMUM PARTICIPANTS: 25

COST: **$95**

ORGANIZER: Tisha Broska

CONTACT: *tisha@nmwild.org*

PAULA EASTWOOD

GUIDED HIKE

Cerro del Yuta (Ute Mountain)

DATE: June 14

DESCRIPTION: Ute Mountain is a proposed wilderness area within the newly designated Rio Grande del Norte National Monument. Ute Mountain sits in Taos County and is managed by the Bureau of Land Management (BLM). For the hike, our group will enter on the north face of Ute Mountain, approaching from the Colorado-New Mexico border. Since no developed trail system is in place, we will utilize game trails to scale the mountain. We will have beautiful views of the southern Rocky Mountains in

View of Rio Grande del Norte National Monument from Ute Mountain

southern Colorado.

BLM ranger Daniel Rael will act as an interpreter to give detailed geological information about the area located in the Wild Rivers Recreation Area within the Taos Plateau.

HIKE LEADERS: John Olivas, traditional community organizer for the New Mexico Wilderness Alliance and Daniel Rael, BLM ranger at Wild Rivers Recreation Area.

HIKING DISTANCE: 4-6 miles roundtrip

HIKING TIME: 6-8 hours

DIFFICULTY: Moderate to difficult with an elevation rise of about 2,500 feet.

DIRECTIONS: Meet at 8 a.m. at the gas station at the junction of N.M. 522 and N.M. 196 in Costilla, approximately 20 miles north of Questa.

NOTE: Suggested items to bring include water, snacks and lunch; sunscreen; camera and binoculars; a hat; good walking shoes and a walking stick.

CONTACT: John Olivas, *john@nmwild.org* or 575-387-2665 or 505-379-5551(cell).

WILD EARTH LLAMA ADVENTURES

COLUMBINE HONDO WILDERNESS STUDY AREA

Columbine Canyon

GUIDED HIKE

DATE: July 12

DESCRIPTION: Come join the New Mexico Wilderness Alliance on a hike in the Columbine Hondo Wilderness Study Area (WSA). Local groups and the conservation community are currently working to convert the Columbine Hondo WSA into true wilderness. Legislation has been introduced, and supporters are needed to keep the federal delegation informed about the importance of this landscape and its protection.

The hike will begin at the Columbine Campground in the Carson National Forest and take us up Columbine Canyon. Elevation change will be from 7,800 feet to approximately 8,800 feet. Bring your walking shoes and plenty of water and join us for this fabulous outing.

HIKE LEADER: John Olivas, traditional community organizer

HIKING DISTANCE: 6 miles

DIRECTIONS: From Questa take N.M. 38 east 5.1 miles to Columbine Campground. Turn right into the campground and go to the Columbine Canyon Trailhead.

CONTACT: *john@nmwild.org* or 575-387-2665 or 505-379-5551.

Bear Trap Canyon Full Moon Campout

DATE: July 18–20

DESCRIPTION: The San Mateo Mountains are one of the most remote landscapes that can be explored in the Cibola National Forest. Absence of any significant human development within or near the range has helped to keep the mountains remote and natural. In particular, the scenery found throughout Bear Trap Canyon is exceptional, with numerous open canyons to explore, high ridgelines that offer dramatic views and an abundance of opportunities to be alone and experience wildness. This region is also rich in wildlife, with mule deer, elk, turkey, black bear, and mountain lions all active in the region.

We will basecamp at Bear Trap Canyon Campground and spend our days exploring Panther Canyon and Chimney Canyon.

MAXIMUM PARTICIPANTS: 10

HIKE LEADER: Nathan Newcomer, Gila grassroots organizer

HIKING DISTANCE: 6–10 miles over two days

CONTACT: *nathan@nmwild.org*

NATHAN NEWCOMER

RYAN HEFFERNAN

Llama Trek in Columbine Hondo

DATE: August 2

DESCRIPTION: Wild Earth Llama Adventures is partnering with the New Mexico Wilderness Alliance on a llama trip into the Columbine Hondo Wilderness Study Area, Columbine Hondo Canyon. Legislation has been introduced by the New Mexico federal delegation to protect the Columbine Hondo as true wilderness.

The *Take a Llama to Lunch!* wilderness day hike is a great way to experience the unspoiled wilderness near Taos. This signature llama trek offers a taste of the wilderness for those who would like to spend a very special day hiking and exploring in the majestic Sangre de Cristo Mountains with experienced guides and wooly hiking companions.

On the trail, our gentle, sure-footed llamas will carry your gear while experienced naturalist guides share their knowledge of southern Rocky Mountain ecology: native flora and fauna, edible and medicinal plants, natural and regional history, and wilderness living skills.

After an inspiring hike at your own pace, you will enjoy a sumptuous feast prepared by the guides in a pristine wilderness setting with some of the most spectacular scenery in the Southwest. Our llamas pack in all the fresh ingredients to make a magnificent gourmet lunch complete with fresh fruits and garden salads, hearty sandwiches on fresh baked breads, natural sodas and delicious desserts to tempt your sweet tooth.

MAXIMUM PARTICIPANTS: 12 (all ages and fitness levels accommodated)

COST: **$99 per person, including lunch**

HIKE LEADER: Wild Earth Llama Adventures

CONTACT FOR HIKE:
tisha@nmwild.org

Gila Wilderness Inventory Workshops 1 & 2

WORKSHOP

DATES: August 9-10 and September 13-14

DESCRIPTION: This year marks the 90th anniversary of America's first wilderness—the Gila. In honor of this momentous occasion, we are hosting a series of workshops to train citizens on how to conduct wilderness inventories in the Gila National Forest, as well as how to conduct citizen monitoring in wilderness areas. Among other things, participants will:

- Learn how to operate GPS software and use it to collect data
- Learn how to perform a wilderness inventory and evaluation
- Learn how to identify signs of wildlife
- Learn how to monitor human impacts in wilderness
- Gain a greater understanding of Forest Service directives and regulations

As a part of the workshop, participants will be provided with a detailed handbook in advance and will spend a full day conducting fieldwork in the Gila National Forest in order to gain a better understanding of the training.

MAXIMUM PARTICIPANTS: 10

LEADER: Nathan Newcomer, Gila grassroots organizer

CONTACT: *nathan@nmwild.org*

PAULA EASTWOOD

Using GPS units in the field

PROJECTS & HIKES

Roadless Area Inventory/ Agua Piedra Creek

VOLUNTEER SERVICE PROJECT

DATE: August 15-17

DESCRIPTION: Arrive Friday for dinner and camp two nights at Agua Piedra Campground on N.M. 518 in Tres Ritos. On Saturday, take an easy hike 2 miles up Agua Piedra Creek through the proposed Special Management Area to the boundary of the northern Santa Barbara Roadless area. Hikers may continue on a strenuous hike (an additional 7.5 miles with 2,000-plus-foot elevation gain) through the roadless area ending at Santa Barbara Campground. A shuttle will be provided from Santa Barbara campground back to Agua Piedra.

MAXIMUM PARTICIPANTS: 15

HIKE LEADER: Cinny Green, *cinny@cinnygreen.com*, www.trailwriters.com

HIKING DISTANCE:
Easy hike-4 miles round trip.
Strenuous hike-9.5 miles.

HIKING TIME: Easy hike-4 hours.
Strenuous hike-9 hours.

CONTACT: John Olivas, *john@nmwild.org*

NOTE: Fees for camping. RV sites available. Bring GPS, camera and/or notebook for inventory. Bring drinking water, snacks, breakfast and lunch food.

PAUL BARDWELL

PROJECTS & HIKES

Wildlife in the Early Hours—Early Bird Sees the Animals!

GUIDED HIKE

DATE: August 19

DESCRIPTION: Wildlife is always most active in the early hours. Can you get up early enough to see them? Join area experts to learn more about animals like mule deer, javelina and elusive desert pronghorn antelope—and hopefully see some of them in their beautiful native habitats! We will hike into the Sierra de Las Uvas grasslands.

HIKE LEADERS: Fernando Clemente and Nathan Small

HIKING DISTANCE: 4 miles

CONTACT: *nathan.p.small@gmail.com*

BUREAU OF LAND MANAGEMENT

Monsoon Wildflower Explosion

GUIDED HIKE

DATE: August 23

DESCRIPTION: Late summer monsoons bring a desert and grassland flower bonanza with them. We'll travel to some of the most beautiful stands that are hidden away in the Sierra de Las Uvas grasslands. These verdant landscapes are some of the most important bird, animal and plant habitats anywhere in southern New Mexico, and you'll be our guest as we see them in what is hopefully full bloom!

HIKE LEADER: Angel Peña

HIKING DISTANCE: 3 miles

CONTACT: *angeldigs@gmail.com*

FLOWER: PAULA EASTWOOD, LANDSCAPE: PAUL BARDWELL

Pecos Wildernes
Gallinas Trail

DATE: August 24

DESCRIPTION: This trail in the Hermits Peak area follows the beautiful Gallinas River upstream to its headwaters at 11,661 feet. Enjoy fields of wildflowers, mushrooms and cascading water along the river before climbing to Burro Canyon. The trail is lightly used with small water crossings along the first 3 miles so wear good waterproof hiking boots. Bring lots of water, lunch, a camera and rain gear. Experts will share botanical and natural history information along the way.

MAXIMUM PARTICIPANTS: 12

HIKE LEADER: Ben Gillock, Hermits Peak Wilderness Area

HIKE DISTANCE: 8.5 miles roundtrip

DIFFICULTY: Moderate to strenuous

CONTACT: Carol Johnson, *carolj@cybermesa.com*

GUIDED HIKE

GARRETT HANKS

Kitchen Mesa at Ghost Ranch

PAULA EASTWOOD

DATE: September 13

DESCRIPTION: Come explore this magical high desert hike through red rock formations in the heart of Georgia O'Keefe country. Stand above Ghost Ranch with views to Abiquiú Lake and the iconic Pedernal. Linger after the hike to explore on your own.

MAXIMUM PARTICIPANTS: 12

HIKE LEADER: Mark Allison

HIKE DISTANCE: 5 miles

ALTITUDE RANGE: 6,500 feet to 7,100 feet (total gain 600 feet).

HIKE TIME: 3-4 hours, though participants could spend additional time exploring Ghost Ranch on their own.

TO REGISTER FOR ANY NM WILD EVENT:
Go to www.nmwild.org

HIKE & PROJECT CANCELLATION POLICY:
Trip cancellations made at least one month in advance of the trip departure are eligible for a full refund. If for any reason we cancel a trip, we will also give a full refund.

View of Cerro Pedernal and Abiquiú Lake from the top of Kitchen Mesa

DIFFICULTY: Moderate (includes a 15-foot chimney through cleft in cliff). The hike is manageable by anyone who is reasonably fit.

DRIVING TIME: Ghost Ranch is located 65 miles northwest of Santa Fe (40 miles beyond Española) on U.S. 84 between mileposts 224 and 225. Allow at least two and a half hours from Albuquerque, one hour and a half from Santa Fe.

COST: **$25 for non-members, $15 for members.** This fee includes your entrance into Ghost Ranch.

CONTACT: *mark@nmwild.org*

NATHAN NEWCOMER

Wilderness Ranger Week
Blue Range Wilderness

DATE: October 5–10

DESCRIPTION: Have you ever wondered what it would be like to be a wilderness ranger working for the U.S. Forest Service? Well, here's your chance to find out, all while experiencing some of the most remote wildlands in southwestern New Mexico, as well as giving back to the land by performing several tasks.

As a part of our continuing series of events in conjunction with the U.S. Forest Service to celebrate the 50th anniversary of the Wilderness Act, we are offering a trip into the heart of the Blue Range Wilderness. The Forest Service will provide pack mules to carry in most of our gear, food and tools. We will be performing various tasks that range from cleaning up campsites to blazing trails and surveying for invasive species. Expect cool days, but that you will be performing actual work to improve the recreational experience of the wilderness.

Join us on this one-of-a-kind outing as you learn what it's like to be a wilderness ranger!

MAXIMUM PARTICIPANTS: 10

US FOREST SERVICE

HIKE LEADER: Nathan Newcomer, Gila grassroots organizer

HIKING DISTANCE: 30–40 miles over five days

CONTACT: *nathan@nmwild.org*

Discover the Chaco Phenomenon

PAULA EASTWOOD

Casa Rinconada

DATE: October 10

DESCRIPTION: Learn about the mysteries and theories of Chaco Culture National Historical Park during a driving and walking tour around the Canyon Loop Drive with an expert archaeologist. The trip will inspire your imagination to travel into the ancient past as we stop at sites like Pueblo Bonito and Casa Rinconada and learn about the ancient pueblo culture. Participants may elect to spend the night in the Gallo campground within Chaco Park.

MAXIMUM PARTICIPANTS: 8

TRIP LEADER: Mark Allison

TRIP DISTANCE: We will drive the Chaco Canyon Loop, stopping at sites for a short walk.

TRIP TIME: The driving/walking tour of Chaco is five hours. This includes time for a picnic lunch. The drive time is six hours roundtrip. People need to plan for an 11-hour day total with driving from Bernalillo.

DRIVING DISTANCE: Approximately three hours one way from our meeting place in Bernalillo.

CONTACT: *mark@nmwild.org*

REGISTRATION FEE: **The cost of the tour is $100 per person.** The fee includes roundtrip transportation from Bernalillo, lunch and snacks.

Thank God, they cannot cut down the clouds!

—Henry David Thoreau

THE WILDERNESS ACT OF 1964 established the National Wilderness Preservation System to preserve the last remaining wildlands in America. The Wilderness Act secures an enduring resource of wilderness for the people. As we celebrate the 50th anniversary of the Wilderness Act in 2014, let's honor the vision and dedication of those who created it by protecting the wilderness we still have left.

WIKIMEDIA COMMONS/JOHN FOWLER

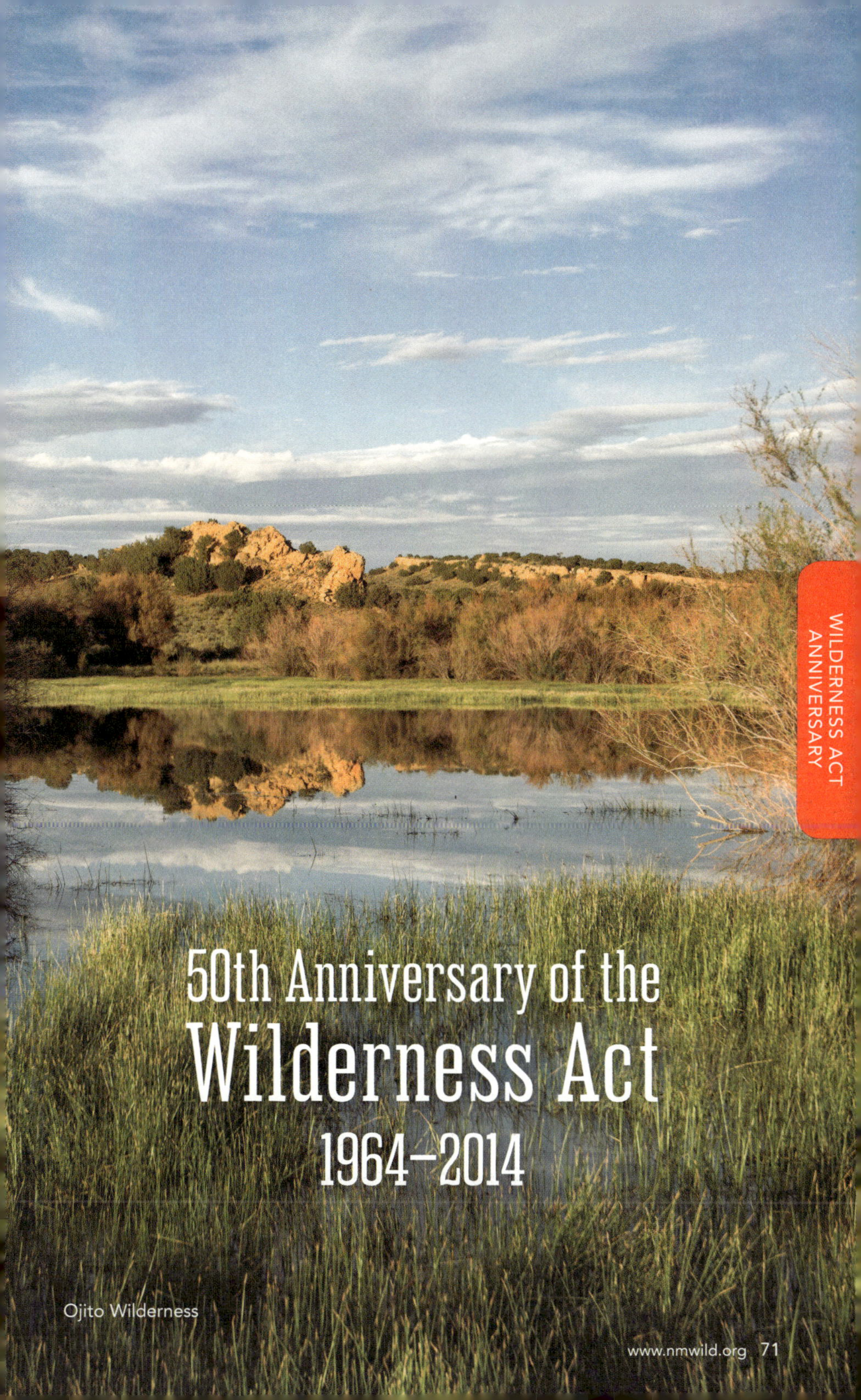

50th Anniversary of the Wilderness Act

1964–2014

Ojito Wilderness

San Pedro Parks Wilderness

NATHAN NEWCOMER

Wilderness50

CELEBRATING 50 YEARS OF AMERICAN WILDERNESS

This year marks the 50th anniversary of the Wilderness Act. To commemorate this important landmark, the New Mexico Wilderness Alliance (NM Wild) joins a handful of local and national organizations to bring to Albuquerque the Wilderness50 National Wilderness Conference on October 15-19.

The National Wilderness Conference will be a historic four-day event of diverse programs, including presentations, panels, exhibits, field trips, skill-development workshops and opportunities to share information about recent advances and emerging issues in wilderness stewardship. Field trips to nearby wilderness areas will be a key component of this year's conference. The companion Wilderness Celebration Exhibition will showcase organizational booths surrounding the Wilderness Interpretive Trail for students and will be open to the public. The conference will close with a Wilderness Festival at Civic Plaza that is open to the public.

The goals for the conference include:

- Making the concept of wilderness and its ecological, recreational, aesthetic, spiritual and symbolic values better known to a wider segment of the American public;
- Providing a forum for discussing the growing challenges of perpetuating the values of wilderness in a time of unprecedented environmental and social change;

The event will include the Wilderness 50 Festival, a family-friendly, community event focused on the history, science and experience of wilderness. It will be an interactive day of hands-on wilderness related activities, as well as an event filled with art, music, storytelling and performances that highlight the various cultures in New Mexico. This festival will celebrate wilderness and the community's connections to our lands, while strengthening stewardship, education and civic engagement.

Conference Information

WHEN: October 15-19, 2014

WHERE: Hyatt Regency Downtown, 330 Tijeras Ave NW **and Albuquerque Convention Center,** 20 First Plaza

REGISTER ONLINE:
www.wilderness50th.org/
conference

SESSION TOPICS:
History
Stewardship
Education
Experience
Civic Engagement
Science for Wilderness

OCTOBER 18 AT 2:00 PM
Wilderness50 Festival— Get Wild to Celebrate our Public Lands!
Civic Plaza, Albuquerque

Wilderness: AMERICA'S LEGACY

BY EMMA TOMINGAS-HATCH

"A wilderness, in contrast with those areas where man and his own works dominate the landscape, is hereby recognized as an area where the earth and its community of life are untrammeled by man, where man himself is a visitor who does not remain."

—From the Wilderness Act of 1964

It has often been said that the wild lands, rugged mountains and open plains are America's legacy; they are what make America and its people unique. Our ancestors and the harsh unforgiving wilderness they managed to survive in have become the stuff of our legends, our heroes and our heritage. However, during the 1900s people began to notice that the very thing that shaped America and its citizens, the wilderness, was now dwindling fast, and conservationists began the fight to save the wild lands of America's natural landscape.

The fight to preserve wilderness areas for future generations has been a long one, taking shape for the first time in 1872 when Yellowstone National Park was established as the first national park in the world. However, even with President Ulysses S. Grant's signature on the Act of Dedication, the effort to preserve the natural beauty of the area was not without obstacles. Yellowstone's remote location meant that only the truly courageous and wealthy could afford the trip to brave the elements. It wasn't until the railroad and automobile made the park easily accessible in 1918 that the area saw a surge of all kinds of visitors.

With the success of Yellowstone and the increasing awareness of other natural wonders in our country, people began actively campaigning for the preservation of America's wilderness. Aldo Leopold, often considered the "Father of Wilderness," took the lead and was instrumental in establishing America's first wilderness area in 1924: the Gila Wilderness in New Mexico. Leopold continued to advocate for the conservation of America's native land, and, in 1935 when the Wilderness Society was formed, he became one of the founding members. Conservation groups continued to promote and fight for wilderness areas but quickly became frustrated with the government's response. Between 1939 and 1964, the total acreage protected by the Forest Service for wilderness purposes only increased by 2 percent, and the boundaries of areas established as protected were constantly being redrafted in order to open heavily wooded areas to the logging industry, according to Doug Scott's 2004 book, "The Enduring Wilderness." Conservationists watched as precious tracts of old growth forests were logged while barren and rocky outcrops were reclassified as wilderness in order to compensate for the removal of the woodlands.

In 1945 Howard Zahniser, a writer and public relations specialist for the U.S. Department of Agriculture's Biological Survey, took the position of executive secretary for the Wilderness Society. He later became the executive director, and in 1951 he began working on drafting what would later become the Wilderness Act. He surveyed conservation groups and spoke at conferences in order to get a consensus of what this potential bill would absolutely need to contain to be an effective law. In June 1956 he had the bill finished and it was introduced in the Senate by Sen. Hubert Humphrey and in House by Rep. John P. Saylor, according to Scott. It wasn't until eight years later in 1964 that Zahniser's hard work finally paid off and the bill was passed. Unfortunately, Zahniser passed away only four months before the Wilderness Act was signed by President Lyndon B. Johnson. The Wilderness Act established the National Wilderness Preservation System, immediately designating the first 9.14 million protected acres. Today the act protects nearly 110 million acres of wilderness throughout America.

The New Mexico Wilderness Alliance (NM Wild) was established in 1997, when members of the New Mexico Wilderness Coalition decided they wanted to make some changes to the organization. The main concern was that there were many areas in New Mexico dubbed as Wilderness Study Areas (WSAs) that had remained so for decades, never becoming officially protected areas of wilderness. The newly formed alliance sought to change that. Its main mission was to "start a program of wilderness protection, research, and public education." In the beginning, the organization was all volunteer based and it wasn't until 1999 that the alliance hired its first fulltime staff person, Edward Sullivan. Through the efforts of hardworking volunteers, members and employees, NM Wild has grown tremendously over the years. Along with working tirelessly for continued protection of wild animals and established wilderness areas in New Mexico, the alliance also has helped two more areas win wilderness designation: the Ojito Wilderness in 2005 and the Sabinoso Wilderness in 2009. NM Wild currently is fighting to establish several wilderness areas within New Mexico, as well as protect wilderness quality lands through administrative methods within the land management agencies' management plans. Read more about our campaigns on pages 10-37.

It has been a long fight for wilderness in this country but a lot of progress has been made and will continue to be made thanks to American citizens who remain passionate about preserving their natural heritage.

Aldo Leopold

AND HIS INFLUENCE ON OUR LAND ETHIC

BY NATHAN NEWCOMER

Land ethic—although not entirely a new concept at the time, Aldo Leopold coined the phrase in his notable book, *A Sand County Almanac*. Now the idea of a land ethic has in and of itself become a guiding philosophy for those who work on wilderness and wildlife conservation in the modern era.

In the early 20th century, forester Leopold noticed that the U.S. Forest Service's land ethic centered on how many acre-board-feet of lumber could be cut every year and how many head of cattle could graze vast grasslands found throughout the Gila National Forest. This form of land ethic based on economics greatly disturbed Leopold. For he was able to see that such a system was on a fast track to eliminating not only the so-called "resources," but also the inherent integrity of the ecological community. As author Philip Connors wrote in his book, *Fire Season: Field Notes from a Wilderness Lookout*, Leopold recognized that "wild nature had a right to existence entirely separate from all human claims, whether economic, cultural, or scientific." In other words, the land has a right to exist for its own sake.

In *A Sand County Almanac*, published in 1949, Leopold laid the foundation for what this land ethic was, and how human beings are an intricate part of the community as a whole:

"The land ethic simply enlarges the boundaries of the community to include soils, waters, plants, and animals, or collectively: the land.

"This sounds simple: do we not already sing our love for and obligation to the land of the free and the home of the brave? Yes, but just what and whom do we love? Certainly not the soil, which we are sending helter-skelter downriver. Certainly not the waters, which we assume have no function except to turn turbines, float barges, and carry off sewage. Certainly not the plants, of which we exterminate whole communities without batting an eye. Certainly not the animals, of which we have already extirpated many of the largest and most beautiful species. A land ethic of course cannot prevent the alteration, management, and use of these 'resources,' but it does affirm their right to continued existence, and, at least in spots, their continued existence in a natural state.

"In short, a land ethic changes the role of *Homo sapiens* from conqueror of the land-community to plain member and citizen of it. It implies respect for his fellow-members, and also respect for the community as such."

Through the leadership and vision of Leopold, applying the land ethic came to mean securing permanent

ABOVE: ALDO LEOPOLD FOUNDATION

protection for a vast swath of national forest in southwestern New Mexico, where at the time Leopold was the head ranger. What this looked and sounded like back in those days was deemed by many to be radical and counterintuitive to the purposes of the Forest Service. However, Leopold persevered and, in 1922, submitted a proposal to the regional office of the Forest Service in Albuquerque requesting that 755,000 acres be set aside as the Gila Wilderness. It wasn't until two years later, on June 3, 1924, that the designation of the Gila Wilderness was officially approved.

Nearly 20 years after Leopold's death in 1948, the United States Congress passed the Wilderness Act of 1964, thereby officially designating America's first wilderness—the Gila. (Since there was no way to congressionally designate areas as "wilderness" in 1924, it had to be administratively designated at the agency level, and thus it remained an agency designation until Congress passed the Wilderness Act in 1964.) This act by Congress also created the National Wilderness Preservation System, which as of today encompasses more than 100 million acres throughout the country. Though Leopold was not there to mark this momentous occasion, it was largely due to his leadership and vision that we are now blessed to experience wild places as they are, and it is this lasting legacy that Leopold left to us to defend and uphold.

U.S. Senator Tom Udall

FOR MANY YEARS, MY PARENTS KEPT A GLASS-ENCLOSED COFFEE TABLE IN THEIR LIVING ROOM IN SANTA FE filled with the pens used by congressmen and President Lyndon Johnson to sign the Wilderness Act of 1964. As secretary of the interior, my dad, Stewart Udall, was a champion of that landmark legislation.

In 2014, we celebrate the 50th anniversary of the Wilderness Act. We take special pride in the act here in New Mexico. In 1924, thanks to the vision of Aldo Leopold, the Gila National Forest was officially designated as a wilderness area—the first in the nation.

The Gila is a pivotal chapter in the conservation movement—a way of looking at the world that has changed the world.

The Gila is a place we all treasure. It is rich in history. We hike its trails and follow legendary footprints, from Geronimo to Ben Lilly, from the Mogollon and Apache to Spanish explorers and prospectors in search of gold. We gaze on its amazing vistas—places like Raw Meat Canyon and Grave Canyon. And we hear the echoes of a storied past.

My dad said that the Wilderness Act of 1964 was one of the most important achievements during his tenure as secretary of the interior: "It is a gift that generations to come will continue to enjoy and fight to protect." The New Mexico Wilderness Alliance is part of that legacy.

Thanks to your efforts, and to so many others who came before us, we will continue to enjoy these beautiful landscapes that enrich our lives and our state.

U.S. Senator Martin Heinrich

SEPTEMBER 3, 2014, MARKS THE 50th ANNIVERSARY OF THE WILDERNESS ACT. In 1964, President Lyndon Johnson signed this historic bill into law after Sen. Clinton P. Anderson of New Mexico managed its passage on the floor of the United States Senate. Having Sen. Anderson shepherd this landmark conservation law through the Senate couldn't have been more appropriate since New Mexico is, on many levels, the birthplace of federal wilderness policy. It was here, after all, that Aldo Leopold successfully saw the Gila Wilderness set aside administratively in 1924 in order to ensure a roadless and backcountry experience free of "Ford dust" for those hearty enough to saddle up or hike into the heart of that wild country.

New Mexico is where the idea of tribally administered wilderness became a reality when Blue Lake was returned to Taos Pueblo. And New Mexico saw the creation of one of the first Bureau of Land Management (BLM) wilderness areas, the Bisti/De-Na-Zin Wilderness, which helped lay the groundwork for a whole system of National Conservation Lands administered by the BLM.

Today, New Mexico is a state where hunters and fishermen, campers and acequia parciantes, chile farmers and urban dwellers all benefit from the recreation, wildlife and water that our wilderness areas provide. As a former outfitter guide and a passionate backcountry sportsman, I, too, know firsthand what these places have meant for New Mexico's culture, economy and history.

But this 50th anniversary celebration isn't just about the past. There is more work to be done to write the story of New Mexico's wilderness areas and wild lands. Broad coalitions have formed to defend and protect special places like the Columbine Hondo in Taos County and the Organ, Potrillo and Las Uvas mountains in Doña Ana Country. The future of wilderness areas across New Mexico will depend on the continued collaborative efforts of our communities, elected officials and organizations like the New Mexico Wilderness Alliance that work tirelessly to protect our treasured natural landscape. I look forward to continued partnership in this effort as we work toward the next 50 years of New Mexico's wilderness legacy.

Wilderness Areas in New Mexico

View towards Apache Kid Wilderness from The Parks

NATHAN NEWCOMER

New Mexico's 25 Wilderness Areas
Cruces Basin
Farmington
Latir Peak
Wheeler Peak
Taos
Chama River Canyon
Bisti/ De-Na-Zin
San Pedro Parks
Bandelier
Pecos
25
Dome
Santa Fe
Sabinoso
Ojito
Gallup
Sandia Mountain
40
Albuquerque
Santa Rosa
West Malpais
Cebolla
Manzano Mountain
25
Withington
Bosque del Apache
Blue Range
Apache Kid
Capitan Mountains
Salt Creek
Roswell
Gila
Aldo Leopold
White Mountain
Silver City
Carlsbad
10
Las Cruces
Carlsbad Caverns
Forest Service
National Park Service
Fish and Wildlife
Bureau of Land Management
0 25 50 75 100
Miles

Pecos Wilderness

Nambé Lake

BY EMMA TOMINGAS-HATCH

YEAR ESTABLISHED: 1964

DESCRIPTION: Some 223,333 acres in the northern half of the state make up the Pecos Wilderness. Nearby are the village of Pecos, the historic town of Las Vegas and New Mexico's state capital, Santa Fe. The Pecos Wilderness is part of the Santa Fe National Forest and is managed by the U.S. Forest Service.

This wilderness area is made up of a vast array of landscapes. The Sangre de Cristo Mountains, which are the southernmost part of the world-famous Rocky Mountains, create a mountainous terrain along the western part of the wilderness, complete with many treacherous ridges, spectacular cliffs, waterfalls (some more than 100 feet high) and peaks towering above timberline. In contrast, the eastern side of the wilderness boasts the Pecos River Valley as well as many gentle streams, grassy meadows, broad flat mesas and fields of wildflowers that are best seen in July and August.

The Pecos Wilderness is home to many different species of wildlife. Most significantly, it hosts one of America's most successful herds of Rocky Mountain bighorn sheep.

There are also deer, elk, turkey and bear. The Pecos Wilderness is also well known for its fishing. It has a vast system of streams, the Pecos River and at least 15 lakes that are available for the sport. The most common types of fish species found in the area are rainbow trout, brown trout and the New Mexico state fish, the Rio Grande cutthroat trout.

In the summer the common activities besides fishing are camping and hiking. There is an immense trail system with something for every level of hiker. There are plenty of easy to access day hikes and also a variety of extended backpacking trails.

WEATHER AND PRECAUTIONS: As always, remember to bring plenty of sunscreen and water, as well as layers of cold weather gear as you may encounter much cooler temperatures in higher altitudes.

DIRECTIONS: The Pecos Wilderness can be accessed from many different points. The easiest is to head north from Santa Fe on I-25 and take exit 299 towards Pecos and Glorieta. Take a left at the exit, a right on NM 50 and then a right on NM 63.The ranger station is on the right.

CONTACT:
Pecos–Las Vegas Ranger District
505-757-6121
Office Hours: M-F, 8 a.m.-5 p.m.
Espanola Ranger District
505-753-7331
Office Hours: M-F, 8 a.m.-5 p.m.
Camino Real Ranger District
575-587-2255
Office Hours: M-F, 8 a.m.-5 p.m.

MORE INFORMATION: *www.fs.usda .gov/recmain/santafe/recreation.*

Mora Flats Day Hike

LEVEL: Easy

LENGTH: 8 miles round trip

ELEVATION CHANGE: 100 feet

ACCESS TO TRAILHEAD: From the town of Pecos head north on NM 63 and Forest Road 223 for 23 miles. Forest Road 223 is very rough and not recommended for low-clearance vehicles or RVs. The road ends at the Iron Gate Campground with access to many trailheads, including the Mora Flats Trail.

DESCRIPTION: Mora Flats is a large valley surrounded by heavily forested mountains. The valley is full of meandering streams and features a few tree-shaded campsites. The trail leading to the valley winds along the Rio Mora canyon ridge and is complete with many glorious views before dropping down into the valley.

ADDITIONAL RESOURCES:
www.pecosnewmexico.com/
www.facebook.com/
ProtectingThePecos
www.fs.usda.gov/main/santafe/home

Wheeler Peak Wilderness

BY TINA DEINES

YEAR ESTABLISHED: 1964

DESCRIPTION: The Wheeler Peak Wilderness lies just northeast of Taos adjacent to the Taos Ski Valley. Managed by the U.S. Forest Service, this wilderness is part of the Carson National Forest and totals almost 20,000 acres. The Wheeler Peak Wilderness includes the highest mountain peak in the state; Wheeler Peak stands at 13,161 feet and is part of the rugged Sangre de Cristo Mountains.

The wilderness is a rugged alpine tundra host to a number of different species, including its summer inhabitants—elk, mule deer, golden eagles, songbirds, marmots, chipmunks and pikas. Other residents include mountain lion and black bear. Bighorn sheep use the wind-swept high-elevation tundra year round. Fauna varies by altitude and includes cottonwood, bristlecone pine, Englemann spruce, sub-alpine fir and many species of wildflower.

The wilderness features a number of rivers and alpine lakes containing cutthroat and/or rainbow trout, which are stocked by the New Mexico Department of Game and Fish. Williams Lake, accessible by using the Williams Lake Trail from the trailhead in Taos Ski Valley, is a popular destination with many hikers and their canine companions.

The Wheeler Peak Wilderness has a number of accessible trails, including Horseshoe Lake/East Fork Trail

Capt. George Wheeler, explorer and cartographer

WIKIMEDIA COMMONS

56, Lost Lake Trail 91, Wheeler Peak Trail 90, Williams Lake Trail 62 and Wheeler Peak Summit Trail 67. If you're looking to stand atop Wheeler Peak, there are two main routes: the Wheeler Peak/Bull of the Woods Trail and the Wheeler Peak Summit Trail, constructed in 2011. If you're looking for more solitude and a longer scenic hike (7.3 miles to the summit), take the Bull of the Woods route. When taking this route, start at daybreak in order to get to the summit before afternoon thunderstorms roll in. The Bull of the Woods route offers some great scenic overlooks, including the Red River Overlook. For a fast trip to the summit, try the Wheeler Peak Summit Trail instead—although it contains some challenging switchbacks in its second half, the summit trail can be completed in just a couple hours. Don't expect much privacy though—on a summer day you are likely to pass dozens of hikers via the Wheeler Peak Summit Trail, which originates from the popular Williams Lake Trail (the route to the top is 4.1 miles altogether from the Williams Lake trailhead). You can find more information about these trails on the Forest Service website: *www.fs.usda.gov/carson.*

Most hiking trails lead to the area's

KEN BUSH

View from Wheeler Peak summit

alpine lakes and peaks. For those wandering off the maintained trails, there are a number of other peaks and ridges, including fine Class 3 scrambles. During the winter months snow transforms the Wheeler Peak Wilderness into a prime backcountry skiing destination—but beware because avalanche risk is significant. Backcountry hiking is allowed, but there are also a number of developed campgrounds near the wilderness trailhead access points.

WEATHER AND PRECAUTIONS:

Average annual temperatures range from 80 degrees in the summer to 20 degrees below zero in the winter. The area gets the highest human traffic between July 4 and Labor Day. July and August enjoy nearly daily afternoon showers, so come prepared if you are coming for a late summer hike in these months. Remember, daytime temperatures can drop dramatically with a storm.

Wheeler Peak is known for its lightning. Beware of lightning on the ridge—get off the ridge if you see thunderclouds overhead. To avoid this danger, leave early in the morning for day hikes up Wheeler Peak.

DIRECTIONS:

The nearest town is Taos. There are two primary ways to access the established public trails that go through the Wheeler Peak Wilderness: NM 150 from the west and NM 578 from the north. Find more detailed directions here: *www.summitpost.org/wheeler-peak-wilderness/454069.*

CONTACT:

Carson National Forest
208 Cruz Alta Road
Taos, NM 87571
575-758-6200
www.fs.usda.gov/carson

Chama River Canyon Wilderness

BY KATHRYN COOK

YEAR ESTABLISHED: 1978

DESCRIPTION: The Chama River Canyon Wilderness is located about 50 miles north of Santa Fe, just northwest of Abiquiú. The 50,300-acre wilderness is managed by the U.S. Forest Service and falls within the borders of both the Santa Fe and Carson national forests.

The Chama River, roughly 120 miles long, originates in Colorado's southern San Juan Mountains and runs south into New Mexico until it merges with the Rio Grande north of Española. Just upstream from Abiquiú, a 6-mile section of the river is surrounded by the Chama River Canyon Wilderness. In 1978, Congress established the wilderness area, which doesn't actually include the Chama River. Instead, a 24.6-mile stretch of the river south of El Vado Dam is protected under the Wild and Scenic Rivers Act (1988). It is managed by both the Forest Service and the U.S. Bureau of Land Management.

The canyon was created by the river as water slowly cut through

the sandstone and shale rock bed. What is left behind is some of New Mexico's most colorful landscape: Sandstone bluffs rise over both shores of the river—the deepest part of the canyon reaching 1,500 feet—revealing layers of saturated, earthy hues that inspired the famous painter Georgia O'Keeffe.

The river and surrounding canyon create dynamic habitats, providing food and shelter to a vast range of plants and animals. Piñon, juniper, Douglas fir and Ponderosa pine fill the dense forests. The canyon itself, and specifically the shores of the river, have a high diversity of vegetation. Wildlife is plentiful, and mule deer, elk, coyotes, black bear and mountain lion are among the canyon's year-round inhabitants. Permanent resident birds include bald and golden eagles, falcons, owls and hawks. Visitors can also see Canada geese, great blue heron and ducks. The river is best known to anglers for its abundant trout.

The wilderness area is a prime spot for an array of outdoor activities, such as rafting, canoeing, hiking, camping, fishing and nature viewing. The most popular activity by far is on the river itself, which is used extensively for rafting. High season extends from May 1 to Labor Day. Rafting operators typically offer one- to two-day trips, which begin just below El Vado Dam and continue for 31 miles downstream, 6 miles of which winds through the wilderness area. However, most river rafting is allowed by permit only, which is run on a lottery system in the summer through the BLM's Taos Field Office. Day-trippers can put in at Chavez Canyon, found toward the end of Forest Road 151, without a permit.

Although the river cuts right through the heart of the wilderness area, visitors will find that river access is surprisingly limited, especially to the north. Only one boat drop-in point and Forest Road 151 provide access to the southern part of the river.

The wilderness area does not have an extensive official hiking trail system, but the Ojitos Trail offers a chance to explore the varying terrain and experience some of the most picturesque views from the top of Ojitos Canyon. The trailhead, which lies at about 6,330 feet, can be found at the gate of Skull Bridge on Forest Road 151. The trail extends for 10.6 miles round-trip and is rated as easy to moderate. If you are more adventurous and want to hop on the Continental Divide National Scenic Trail, the entry point is also here, at Skull Bridge near the Ojitos trailhead.

Another recommended hike is to simply follow Forest Road 151. Mountain bikers and horseback riders enjoy this route, which follows the canyon. There is also a short, 2.5-mile Rim Vista Trail, which can be found 0.7 miles after turning off U.S. 84 onto Forest Road 151. Otherwise, those more adventurous can follow several of the unmarked (and often incomplete) dirt trails around the wilderness.

Campsites are also abundant, both officially and in the backcountry. Several established sites are close to the river along Forest Road 151. It is recommended that backpackers set up camp away from the fragile river

BUREAU OF LAND MANAGEMENT

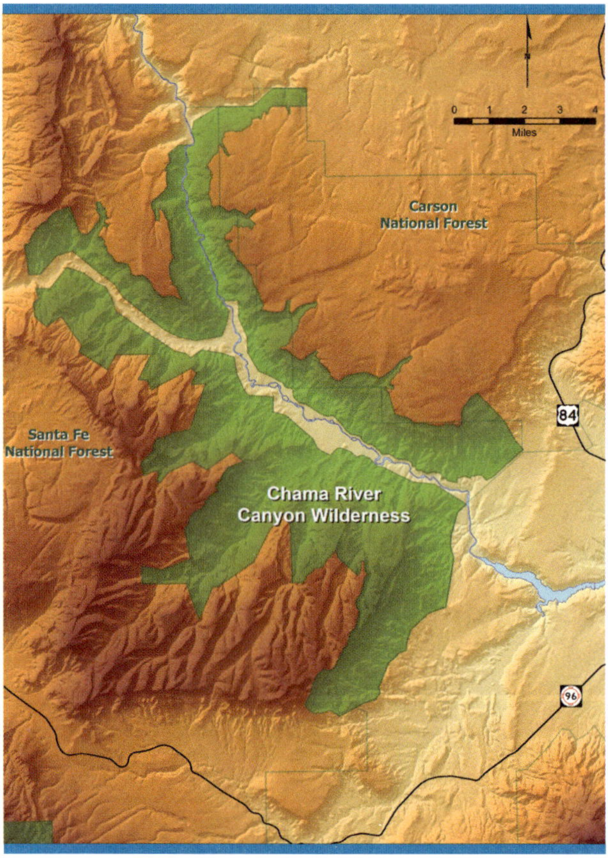

CHAMA RIVER CANYON WILDERNESS

late spring and fall offer more solitude. Winter months are not usually suitable for rafting due to the low water levels. A note of caution: Forest Road 151 is susceptible to wet weather and often impassable when muddy.

DIRECTIONS:

From Española, take U.S. 84 in the direction of Abiquiú. Follow U.S. 84 until you pass Abiquiú and Ghost Ranch Piedra Lumbre Educational and Visitor Center. Turnoff for Forest Road 151 is on the left. This will lead you into the canyon.

shore to avoid damaging the sensitive ecosystem. All visitors are expected to follow the seven rules of Leave No Trace.

Fishing is another popular river activity. Permits from the New Mexico Department of Game and Fish are required.

WEATHER AND PRECAUTIONS:

The Chama River Canyon Wilderness is open year-round, but the high seasons are spring and summer, particularly between May 1 and Labor Day when rafting and summer activities are in full swing. To avoid crowds—and high summer temperatures—

CONTACT:

For Rafting permits:
BLM Taos Field Office
226 Cruz Alta Road
Taos, NM 87571-5983
575-758-8851
River Information Recording:
888-882-6188

MORE INFORMATION:

Coyote Ranger District
HC 78 Box 1
Coyote, NM 87102
Phone: 575-638-5526

Rules in Wilderness

Just because they are wild doesn't mean you can do whatever you want in our state's wilderness areas. In order to protect our wilderness areas in perpetuity, it is important that we act as stewards when we visit. Here is a list of general wilderness rules as outlined at **www.wilderness.net:**

- Motorized equipment and equipment used for mechanical transport is generally prohibited on all federal lands designated as wilderness. This includes the use of motor vehicles, motorboats, motorized equipment, bicycles, hang gliders, wagons, carts and portage wheels as well as the landing of helicopters and other aircraft.

- In a few areas, special regulations allow the use of motorized equipment or mechanical transport. Contact the federal agency that oversees the area for more specific information.

- The Wilderness Act requires management of human-caused impacts and protection of the area's wilderness character to ensure that it is "unimpaired for the future use and enjoyment as wilderness." Use of the equipment listed as prohibited in wilderness is inconsistent with the provision in the Wilderness Act which mandates opportunities for solitude or primitive recreation and that wilderness is a place that is in contrast with areas where people and their works are dominant.

- Also, recognize the principles of Leave No Trace, which are outlined on pages 130-131 of this book.

MORGUEFILE.COM

Sabinoso Wilderness

BY TINA DEINES

Agapito Rim

YEAR ESTABLISHED: 2009

DESCRIPTION: The designation of the Sabinoso Wilderness in 2009 was one of the New Mexico Wilderness Alliance's first conservation successes and was the second wilderness designation in 20 years in New Mexico. This 16,030-acre wilderness rises 1,110 feet from the surrounding plains in northeastern New Mexico and is managed by the U.S. Bureau of Land Management (BLM).

The Sabinoso Wilderness sits upon the Canadian Escarpment, which is composed mostly of the Jurassic Morrison Formation and Triassic Chinle Shale. Cretaceous Dakota Sandstone caps these formations and creates colorful cliffs at the top of the long, deep canyons of the area. The dominant feature is the 1,000-foot-deep Cañon Largo, which connects to the Canadian River just outside the wilderness. Several other narrow canyons feed rainfall and snowmelt into Cañon Largo, while Lagartija Creek drains the southern portion of the wilderness. Elevations range from 4,520 to 6,150 feet.

Fairly dense piñon-juniper

BUREAU OF LAND MANAGEMENT

woodlands dominate the landscape. Ponderosa pines grow in isolated stands on the mesa tops and mix with cottonwood and willow trees along riparian areas in the canyon bottoms. Understory plants here include wavyleaf and shinnery oak, mountain mahogany, netleaf hackberry, skunkbush sumac and Navajo tea. Grasses include black, sideoats, blue and hairy grama; galleta; little bluestem; wolftail; Indian rice grass; and vine mesquite. The area's diversity of habitats, from forests to cliffs to riparian bottomlands, supports a wide variety of birds including red-tailed hawk, American kestrel, western scrub-jay, mourning dove, lesser goldfinch, savannah sparrow, broad-tailed hummingbird, hairy woodpecker, white-throated swift, and turkey vulture. Other wildlife in the area includes coyote, mule deer, bobcat, gray fox, ground squirrel, racer snake and a variety of frogs and butterflies in the riparian zones.

The sharp contrast of densely vegetated mesas with many rocky canyons creates exceptional scenery. These canyons cut up to 1,000 feet into the sandstone rock and have been stained buff, red and tan over the millennia by various oxides. Extended seasons of flowing water, even in fairly dry years, and incredibly broad vistas across the eastern plains add to Sabinoso's scenic appeal. Outstanding recreational opportunities in the area include hunting, hiking, geological study, horseback riding and landscape photography, but access currently is difficult.

ACCESS: The Sabinoso Wilderness is surrounded by private land, and there currently is no public access. The only way to access the area is to make arrangements with the Taos District office of the BLM. The office is making efforts to purchase land and rights-of-ways to gain public access to the area. Please respect private property and do not trespass.

CONTACT:
Taos BLM
505-758-8851

Local Support

Sabinoso was designated as wilderness on March 24, 2009, when President Barack Obama signed the Omnibus Public Lands Management Act. Resolutions in support of protecting Sabinoso came from the San Miguel County Commission, the City of Las Vegas, the regional economic development group and local ranchers.

Apache Kid Wilderness

BY NATHAN NEWCOMER

YEAR ESTABLISHED: 1980

DESCRIPTION: The Apache Kid Wilderness, located in the southern portion of the San Mateo Mountains, is one of the most remote wilderness areas in all of New Mexico. Most of the mountain range is roadless, isolated and natural. Largely due to the size of the area, its topography and vegetative diversity, the Apache Kid Wilderness possesses outstanding opportunities for solitude and unconfined or primitive forms of recreation. Steep slopes in the northern portion of the wilderness pour down into the surrounding canyons, providing for a variety of vegetation, including ponderosa, oak, aspen, spruce and fir, as well as all three major juniper types.

The scenery found throughout the area is exceptional, with numerous open canyons to explore, high ridgelines that offer dramatic views and an abundance of opportunities to be alone and experience wildness. There is a large variety of grasses and wildflowers, including yellow ragweed, purple verbena, sideoats grama, blue grama, burro grass, silver beardgrass, wolftail and purple three-awn.

At 44,650 acres in size, the Apache Kid Wilderness offers some of the wildest country left in the state of New Mexico. Scores of elk can be seen roaming the western flanks; the endangered Mexican spotted owl finds substantial habitat throughout the region; and several years ago, a pair of Mexican gray wolves left the Gila country and were found sustaining themselves off of the local deer population.

The area is named after the Apache Kid, a known renegade during the U.S. military's campaign against Geronimo and his people. Legend states that the young Apache was captured and killed within the present-

NATHAN NEWCOMER

Apache Kid Wilderness, looking northeast to the ramparts of Vick's Peak

day wilderness, though some believe it was another young apache named Massai. Were the Apache Kid to return to the San Mateo Mountains today, he'd find them just as wild as he did 100 years ago—perhaps wilder.

WEATHER AND PRECAUTIONS: Average annual temperatures range between 95 degrees in the summer and 45 degrees in the winter. The area receives relatively little use, except during hunting season, which begins in early September and lasts through late December. Check with the New Mexico Department of Game and Fish for specific dates when hunting is allowed. July and August enjoy nearly daily afternoon showers, so be prepared if you are coming for a late summer hike. Remember, daytime temperatures can drop dramatically with a storm.

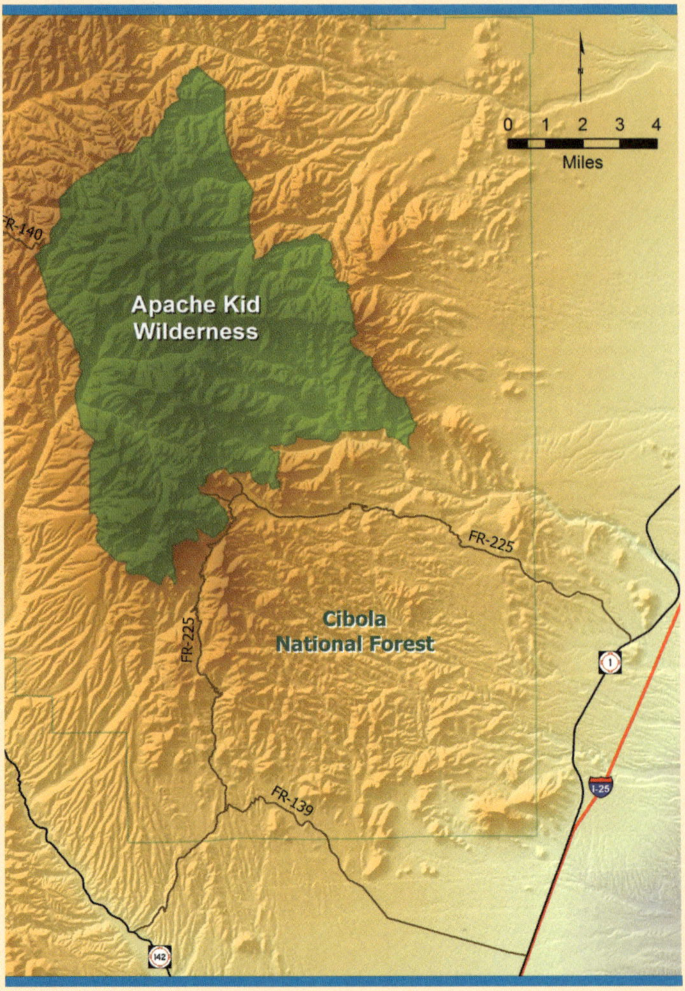

APACHE KID WILDERNESS

Be prepared to carry your own water as well, as there are very few natural springs in the wilderness that can be relied upon.

DIRECTIONS:

The Apache Kid Wilderness is located roughly halfway between Socorro and Truth or Consequences. Primary access to the wilderness is via Forest Road 225, which heads west towards the wilderness from N.M. 1, near Interstate 25. There are two U.S. Forest Service campgrounds adjacent to the wilderness—Springtime Campground and Luna Park—though both sites are primitive and do not provide services.

CONTACT:

Cibola National Forest
Magdalena Ranger District
P.O. Box 45
Magdalena, NM 87825
575.854.2281
www.fs.usda.gov

Lost Outdoors

STAYING "FOUND" AND WHAT TO DO IF LOST

Adapted from the American Hiking Society, www.americanhiking.org

Here are some general tips to help you stay found on the trails:

- Bring a map and compass, even on short day hikes. Even if you know the trail like the back of your hand, snow, fog and darkness may obscure familiar features. A high-quality topographic map is worth every penny.

- Know how to use your map and compass. Know how to find north, how to orient your map to the terrain and how to take a heading.

- Don't rely on GPS. Global Positioning Systems can be hugely helpful, but are vulnerable to mechanical shock and battery failure. Learn to use a map and compass before you decide to rely on GPS. Even then, always bring a compass and map as backup.

- Pay attention. Which side of the trail does the stream run on? Where is the sun in the sky? Did you see that big rock on the way in? If you are returning on the same trail you used on the way in, turn around periodically and look back at the trail, especially where it intersects with another trail or a decommissioned trail. It looks different in reverse!

IF YOU GET LOST:

- Don't panic. The worst possible thing you can do upon realizing you are lost is to panic. It's also a very natural reaction, so be prepared to consciously overcome it.

- Stay calm and take some deep breaths. Odds are that you haven't strayed too far from the path, and by staying calm, you might be able to hear other hikers nearby.

- If you are genuinely lost, stay put. Rescuers will be looking for you where they know you've been hiking. Don't put yourself in more danger by wandering further from a known location. If you do so, you will also be putting rescuers in greater danger as they will have to cover more ground and use more time to locate you. The only time not to stay put would be when it is unsafe to remain where you are, perhaps due to flooding or avalanche potential.

- While it's nothing you should ever rely on, check for a cell phone signal if you have a cell phone. Periodically blow your emergency whistle in bursts of three. Be visible to rescuers—wear or display bright clothing, use a signal mirror, etc. Even your camera's flash can be used to signal your presence.

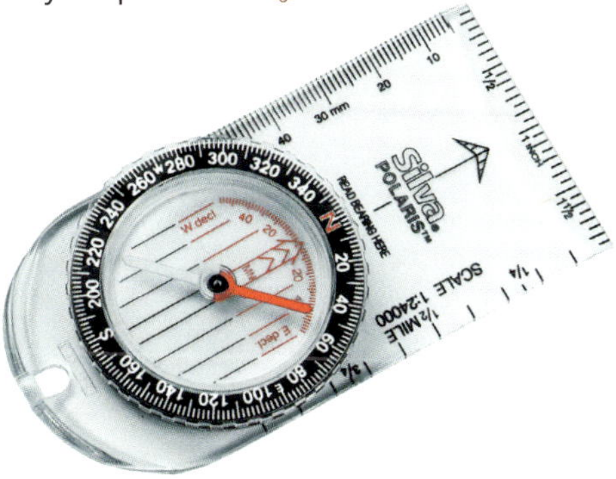

USFS/LINCOLN NATIONAL FOREST

White Mountain Wilderness

BY TINA DEINES

YEAR ESTABLISHED: 1964

DESCRIPTION: The 48,266-acre White Mountain Wilderness lies in Lincoln County about 15 miles northwest of Ruidoso. Located in the Sierra Blanca Mountains (a sub-range of the Sacramento Mountains), it gets its name from the white mountain tops—heavy snow covered peaks can last from late November to June. Elevation ranges from 5,000 to more than 11,000 feet. The wilderness is managed by the U.S. Forest Service.

The area contains four different life zones within its boundaries: piñon-juniper, ponderosa pine, mixed conifer and sub-alpine forest. You can encounter a variety of wildlife here, including mule deer, elk, black bears, wild turkeys, porcupines, badgers, bobcats, foxes, coyotes, skunks, squirrels, mice, voles and rats. Many bird species live in the White Mountain Wilderness, and it's a critical habitat for five of those species: northern three-toed woodpeckers, Clark's nutcrackers, red-breasted nuthatches, Townsend's solitaires and golden-crowned kinglets.

There are about 50 miles of hiking trails, ranging from easy to difficult—most are well marked. Most trails are located in the higher elevations of the wilderness and offer stunning views. The majority of these trails eventually lead to the Crest Trail, a 21-mile long hike through the wilderness.

WEATHER AND PRECAUTIONS: Expect dry, windy conditions during the spring with temperatures ranging from freezing to 80 degrees. The "rainy season" comes during July and August—expect afternoon showers accompanied by high temperatures. Snow typically starts falling around mid-November, averaging 6 feet or more. Winter temperatures average around 22 degrees. While water is not plentiful in this wilderness, it can be found with some diligent searching. Come prepared for the season and conditions.

MORE INFORMATION AND MAP OF TRAILS:

www.fs.usda.gov/attmain/lincoln/specialplaces

DIRECTIONS:

When visiting the White Mountain Wilderness, NM Wild suggests contacting the Smokey Bear Ranger District in Ruidoso ahead of time for maps and directions to accessible trailheads. You can also visit them at the address below.

CONTACT:

Smokey Bear Ranger District
901 Mechem
Ruidoso, NM 88345
575-257-4095

Our Work in the White Mountain Wilderness

BY LYNNE UHRING

The National Forest Foundation funded the New Mexico Wilderness Alliance during 2012 to work with the Lincoln National Forest on improving its Wilderness Stewardship Challenge Inventory scores. The two wilderness areas in the Lincoln are the White Mountain Wilderness and the Capitan Wilderness, both of which lie within the Smokey Bear Ranger District headquartered in Ruidoso.

About half of the White Mountain Wilderness burned in the Little Bear Fire, which jumped containment lines on June 9, 2012, becoming a huge wildfire. The wilderness was closed for more than two months, significantly shortening the time that volunteers were allowed into the wilderness to gather data.

Volunteers found and recorded campsites, stands of the invasive musk and bull thistles, points of interest and natural characteristics. Solitude is important in the wilderness experience. Since solitude is not easily measured, volunteers recorded encounters with other people while they were inside the boundaries of the wilderness. On 21 inventory hikes there were no encounters with other people. Fifty-six encounters with other people occurred during 17 inventory hikes in the White Mountains. Activities of the people encountered included camping, hiking, photography, hunting, horseback riding and backpacking. Sixty-five natural characteristic data points were recorded. Volunteers also recorded natural characteristics including scenic vistas, flowering meadows, cliffs, big trees, cascading water, horned toads, butterflies, big cat paw prints, turkey feathers and bear scat.

Aldo Leopold Wilderness

BY TINA DEINES AND NATHAN NEWCOMER

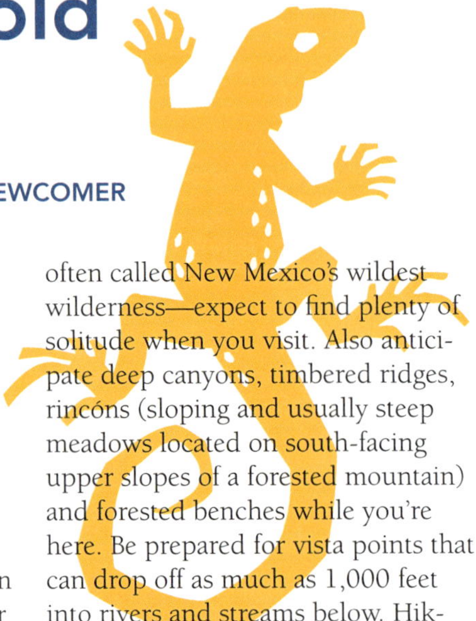

YEAR ESTABLISHED: 1980

DESCRIPTION: The vast canyon and mesa country of the Mogollon, Diablo, Tularosa and Black Mountain ranges in southwestern New Mexico makes up the Gila National Forest. Tucked away on the far eastern portion of this landscape in the Black Range lies the 202,016-acre Aldo Leopold Wilderness—it was named in honor of the man who many consider to be the founding father of wildlife conservation and of the United States' Wilderness Preservation System.

It was through the leadership of Aldo Leopold that the U.S. Forest Service set aside 755,000 acres in the headwaters of the Gila and Mimbres rivers as the world's first wilderness area on June 3, 1924. This marked the first time that a large expanse of woodland was to be preserved in its natural state, and management was wonderfully simple: "Prohibit roads and hotels, and then leave it alone." In many respects, management hasn't changed all that much since then.

The Aldo Leopold Wilderness contains the most rugged and wild portion of the Black Mountain Range, stretching north-south along the crest of the Black Range for about 30 miles. The highest point in the wilderness is McKnight Mountain at 10,165 feet.

Because it is so wild and remote, the Aldo Leopold Wilderness is often called New Mexico's wildest wilderness—expect to find plenty of solitude when you visit. Also anticipate deep canyons, timbered ridges, rincóns (sloping and usually steep meadows located on south-facing upper slopes of a forested mountain) and forested benches while you're here. Be prepared for vista points that can drop off as much as 1,000 feet into rivers and streams below. Hiking and backpacking are the major recreational opportunities in the area, and hunting is permitted. The Continental Divide of the Americas passes through the center ridgeline of the wilderness, and more than 30 miles of the Continental Divide National Scenic Trail (CDT) forms a portion of the southern boundary (with many miles of trails). We suggest devoting a portion of your time to this area.

The fauna is correspondingly varied, with a myriad of wildlife found throughout the region. Several threatened and endangered species, such as the Gila cutthroat trout and Mexican gray wolf, find refuge in the Aldo Leopold Wilderness. Elk, turkey and blue grouse can be found in the high country, along with Gila monsters and rattlesnakes in the low canyon bottoms. Other common wildlife in the region includes bear, bobcats, mountain lions, bats, foxes and ringtail cats, in addition to a multitude of songbirds and various reptiles. This

ANN McMAHON ©2012

wilderness area, along with the Gila Wilderness, is also integral to the Mexican gray wolf re-introduction program. The native Gila trout has been brought back from near extinction and exists in small populations in some of the local watersheds. Local plant life includes juniper, piñon pine and oak at the lower altitudes. Above 7,000 feet, other pines, fir, spruce and aspen dominate the landscape.

WEATHER AND PRECAUTIONS:
Most streams and springs in this wilderness are seasonal and unreliable, so be prepared for a scarcity of water when you visit. Because this wilderness area is used far less than others in the state, most trails are hard to identify, which can cause navigational difficulties. Come prepared with your map and compass! (See "What to do if Lost on the Trail" on page 95 and "Map and Compass with Michael Grady" on pages 48-49 for more tips on navigation).

NOTE: More than 130,000 acres in the Black Range burned during the summer of 2013. The southern portion of the Aldo Leopold Wilderness burned moderately, with some areas burning severely. Check with the local Forest Service Ranger District on current trail and campground conditions.

DIRECTIONS:
Primary access to the Aldo Leopold Wilderness is via N.M. 152 on the southern boundary of the wilderness. Numerous campgrounds and trailheads can be found off the highway. Access to the western half of the wilderness for would-be explorers is via Forest Service Road 150.

CONTACT:
Wilderness Ranger District
HC 68 Box 50
Mimbres, NM 88049
575-536-2250
Black Range Ranger District
1804 N Date St.
Truth or Consequences, NM 87901
575-894-6677

Ojito Wilderness

BY TANIA SOUSSAN

YEAR ESTABLISHED: 2005

DESCRIPTION: The 11,183-acre Ojito Wilderness is special in many ways, not least its ties to the past. Petroglyphs, ruins and artifacts such as Folsom points tell the stories of prehistoric Pueblo, Navajo and Hispanic cultures.

Long ago, the area was covered by inland seas. Erosion over time has exposed bones, large segments of petrified trees and seashells. Today, Ojito is world renowned for its fossil remains of rare dinosaurs, plants, trees and marine invertebrates. Perhaps the most exciting discovery was the skeleton of one of the largest dinosaurs ever found, a Seismosaurus. Do not disturb fossils, petrified wood or archaeological artifacts.

Ojito is a rugged but beautiful high desert landscape with badlands in hues of green, blue and violet; hoodoos reaching as tall as 40 feet; steep

BUREAU OF LAND MANAGEMENT

Ojito Wilderness at dawn

From Wildlands to Wilderness

The designation of the Ojito Wilderness in 2005 was one of the New Mexico Wilderness Alliance's first conservation victories. In the mid-90s, NM Wild formed and established itself as the statewide grassroots voice for wildlands. In the mid-2000s, the organization started pushing for Ojito Wilderness. Efforts included collaboration with the Zia tribe, former New Mexico Gov. Bruce King and other statewide elected officials. After passing both the U.S. House of Representatives (unanimously) and U.S. Senate, the Ojito Wilderness Act was signed into law on Wednesday, October 26, 2005, by President George W. Bush.

canyons and dramatic cliffs.

Experienced hikers and backpackers will find plenty of challenges among the steep-sided mesas, remote box canyons and miles of meandering arroyos. But families with children and others looking for an easy hike will find there is plenty of adventure to be had and sights to be seen—as well as opportunities for solitude—even on shorter walks.

Horseback riding, wildlife observation, bird watching, hunting and fishing also can be enjoyed at Ojito. The colorful rock layers in the canyon walls and cliffs create a stunning panorama for photographers and sightseers, especially at dawn and dusk.

Ojito is home to birds of prey, and swifts and swallows nest there. The wilderness area also provides habitat for various reptiles, mule deer, elk, American antelope and mountain lion. Three rare plant species—grama grass cactus, Knight's milkvetch and Townsend's aster–also are found in

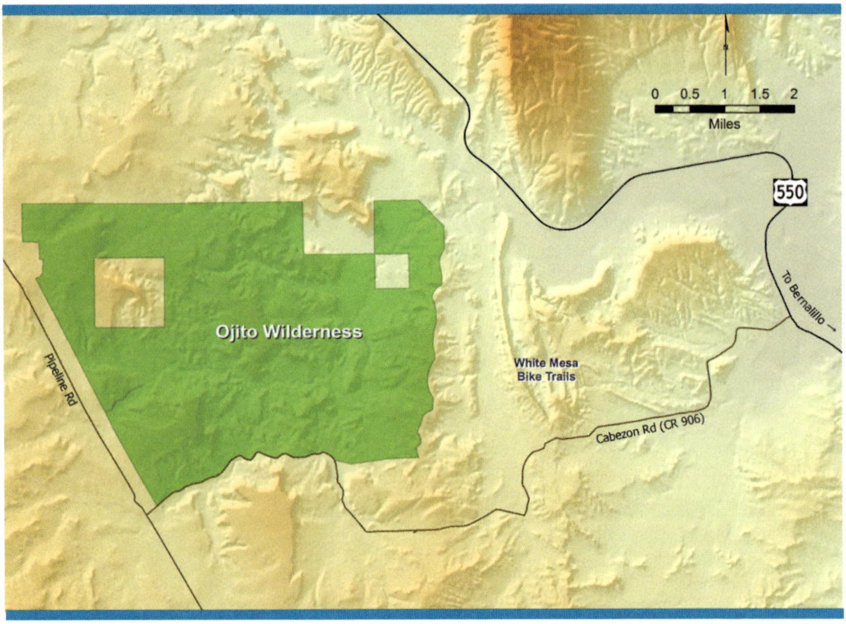

OJITO WILDERNESS

Ojito along with New Mexico's lowest elevation stands of Ponderosa pines.

WEATHER AND PRECAUTIONS:

Average high temperatures in the area range from the low 90s in July to the low 40s in December and January. Low temperatures average 20 degrees in winter, but summer lows average in the 50s.

Dressing in layers is a good idea as weather can be unpredictable. In addition, water is rare at Ojito so bring plenty of your own.

Dirt access roads in the area are passable during dry weather but they can get slippery and rutted during wet seasons. It also is easy to get lost in the hundreds of miles of dirt roads surrounding the wilderness, so pay careful attention to where you are traveling and where you have been. Cell phones don't usually work at Ojito.

The closest facilities are in the Village of San Ysidro, 10 miles away.

DIRECTIONS:

Bernalillo is the closest town to Ojito. Take U.S. 550 northwest toward Cuba for about 20 miles. Approximately two miles before San Ysidro, turn left onto Cabezon Road (County Road 906) and follow the left fork about 10 miles to the wilderness sign.

Some areas within and near the wilderness boundaries are private, state or Zia Pueblo lands. A recreation permit is required to access state lands, and permission is needed to enter or cross private lands.

CONTACT:

Bureau of Land Management
435 Montano NE
Albuquerque, NM 87107
505-761-8700
www.nm.blm.gov

Drink Up

Keep yourself hydrated on and off the trail

BY EMMA TOMINGAS-HATCH

We all know how essential drinking plenty of water is for our everyday health. Your body needs water to clean out toxins, to breathe and even for your brain to function properly. Even slight dehydration can affect your ability to think clearly and alter your mood.

When you are going to be out in the wilderness it is especially important to make sure you bring enough fluids for your trip. Never assume that you will need less water if the weather is cold or cloudy. It is always a good idea to have at least one extra water bottle in your backpack and to try to take small sips frequently throughout the day. Gulping water every few hours is not as effective as taking small, frequent sips because your body needs to continually replace the fluid you are sweating out. A good guideline is to drink a quart of water for every half hour you are hiking.

The best way to make sure you are staying hydrated is to choose a convenient method of carrying your water. For example, a water bladder with a hose is easy and comfortable to carry, and the nozzle is right next to your face so you can access it frequently without having to stop and remove your backpack.

It can be difficult to pack enough water if you are going to be on a long trip so remember to plan your trip around water sources. Of course, when getting your water from a natural source, like a lake, you need to purify it before consuming it. There are a number of ways to do so, such as boiling the water, treating it with iodine or using a water purifier.

If you are planning on hiking longer than an hour it is a good idea to bring a sports drink or rehydration powder to add to your water. These, unlike water, replace the chemicals that are lost through sweat. According to the Cleveland Clinic medical center, losing electrolytes through perspiration can cause problems such as muscle cramping and fatigue.

When packing your supplies keep in mind that fruits and veggies not only make a great healthy trail snack, but a lot of them are full of water as well and a great way to aid your hydration. Here is a list of a few you can take with you on the trail: cucumbers, oranges, grapefruit, watermelon, tomatoes, peaches, radishes and celery.

Nandi near Nambé Lake

Hiking with Dogs

BE PREPARED WHEN YOU TAKE YOUR FOUR-LEGGED FRIEND OUTDOORS.

This guide will help you pack for a hike with your best friend, whether it's nearby or far away. Remember to research the area you will be hiking in ahead of time and be prepared for the conditions. You may have heard recent stories about unprepared hikers leaving their dogs in the mountains because they did not plan ahead for the weather conditions or terrain. Please don't let your pooch down!

IMPORTANT GEAR

- Collar with identification tags
- Leash
- Food and plenty of water
- Collapsible bowl
- Poop bags
- First aid kit
- Reflective jacket or clip-on light
- Doggy jacket for cold weather conditions
- Swamp cooler or cooling bandanna for warm conditions
- Paw protecting balm or booties for rough terrain

OTHER RESOURCES FOR HIKING WITH DOGS

Hiking with Dogs: Becoming a Wilderness-Wise Dog Owner by Linda B. Mullally

The Trail Hound's Handbook: Your Family Guide to Hiking with Dogs by Ellen Eastwood

Left: Rosie wears a figure-flattering chartreuse reflective vest, especially important during hunting season and at dusk.

Right: Daisy wears a sleek mist-gray "swamp cooler" vest for those hot days on New Mexico trails—great for black dogs.

Hike Like a Dog by Tina Deines

Whenever I get packed up to go hiking some of New Mexico's wild lands, it's always my dogs Daisy and Rosie who get the most excited. As we get closer and closer to the mountains, I can hear their excitement when they see the rugged peaks, the trees, the wild. Dogs have a special way of connecting with nature—they take in every scent and every noise, and truly become one with the wild. Watching Daisy and Rosie connect with wilderness is a great reminder of how lucky we as people are to have wild spaces. So next time you get out on the trails, try taking it all in like a dog—every sound, sight and scent!

What Wilderness Means

BY MARK ALLISON, Executive Director

Sabinoso Wilderness

There is "wilderness" and there is "Wilderness." The former (with a lower case "w") refers to areas that are substantially free from the effects of modern civilization, that are essentially natural and undeveloped and that afford excellent opportunities for solitude and "unconfined" recreation such as hiking, camping, cross-country skiing and fishing. They are places where humans visit but don't live. They most likely also have other special features, such as ecologic, geologic, scenic or cultural significance.

The latter (with a capital "W") entails all these characteristics but is federal public land that enjoys a special permanent protected status. This protected status is possible because of the 1964 Wilderness Act.

Only 2 percent of New Mexico's total land area is protected Wilderness. We estimate that there are an additional 4.6 million acres in New Mexico that may qualify and be deserving of protected wilderness designation. Without that formal protection, these special places that New Mexicans care so much about face logging, off-road vehicle use, road building and other threats that would destroy the very things we love about them, not just today but tomorrow and generations into the future.

I fell in love with New Mexico as a third-grader visiting from Illinois and have never doubted the life-changing

ABOVE: BUREAU OF LAND MANAGEMENT

importance of being exposed to our special wild places. Now that I'm a parent I've tried to share that passion with my children at every opportunity I have. Recreation—backpacking, skiing, rafting and snow shoeing—was how I was introduced to wilderness and is still an integral part of how (and where) my family spends our free time.

Wilderness is also important as an idea—to know that there are still a few places that exist that are essentially untouched and "untrammeled" by us—I think that knowledge enriches all of humanity.

But protecting wilderness is about much more than just having a place to have fun, as important as that is. For me personally, it is critical to my physical, mental and emotional health. Getting into the wild makes me a better partner, father and friend (just ask them)! More importantly, protecting wilderness honors our history and our cultural heritage. Protecting wilderness helps our watersheds and air quality and the overall health of our planet. Protecting wilderness provides critical habitat for threatened species and supports biodiversity. Wilderness is also important as an idea—to know that there are still a few places that exist that are essentially untouched and "untrammeled" by us. I think that knowledge enriches all of humanity, whether we personally visit it or not. You no doubt have your own thoughts about why wilderness matters.

New Mexico has a rich and proud legacy of protecting wild places and played a central role in the creation and evolution of the wilderness protection movement itself. The acknowledged "father of wildlife conservation" and a true wilderness visionary, Aldo Leopold, spent 13 of his most formative professional years in New Mexico. Among many other contributions, it was Leopold who was responsible for the administrative designation of New Mexico's Gila as the *world's* first wilderness area in 1924.

Later, New Mexico's Sen. Clinton Anderson introduced and supported numerous pieces of conservation and environmental legislation and was a sponsor of the 1964 Wilderness Act. It has been said that without Clinton Anderson there would have been no wilderness law. New Mexico's influential role in wilderness was recognized again as the Gila became the first congressionally designated wilderness signed into law.

Since then, New Mexico has been blessed by many other authors, thinkers and leaders in wilderness protection, private citizens and elected officials alike. And of course, those of us who are fortunate to call New Mexico home and those of us who visit know how special and important our mountains, deserts and rivers are. We can see in those special places we hold dear the differences between those that are protected and those that are not.

Big Canyon —APTLY NAMED

BY STEVE WEST

Driving south on U.S. 62-180 from Carlsbad toward El Paso, hundreds of thousands of people pass along the eastern escarpment of the Guadalupe Mountains, often with no idea of what is found in those seemingly low-lying mountains. In fact, the Guadalupe Mountains contain two well-known national parks, Carlsbad Caverns and Guadalupe Mountains. While the former includes some of the lower elevation areas, the latter includes the highest areas in addition to the high point in the Guadalupes and the highest peak in Texas. In between is the Lincoln National Forest.

Carlsbad Caverns National Park was first established as a national monument in 1924 and finally as a park six years later. The main draw there is Carlsbad Cavern itself, which has been visited by tens of millions of people. Guadalupe Mountains National Park was established in 1972 to protect the exposed Permian reef and unique plant and animal communities. Fall colors are a major draw to the park with thousands of people visiting McKittrick Canyon—which along with the high point, Guadalupe Peak at 8,749 feet—is probably the best-known site in the park.

The Guadalupes offer excellent

hiking with the only real problem being you have to carry your own water wherever you go. Other than that, you're ready to go! Hiking is great in all seasons, and with the exception of extremely hot or cold days, you can plan your hikes around your own schedule.

My favorite hike is into an area rarely frequented by other people. Big Canyon is the last canyon in New Mexico before you reach the Texas border. Aptly named, it is the second largest canyon in the 70-mile stretch of mountains. The best way to visit the canyon used to be to drive along a series of very rough dirt roads to the mouth and then walk up the canyon. Much of the entrance is Bureau of Land Management land and after a short time walking up the canyon you would enter the Lincoln National Forest. A small patch of private land at the entrance now makes it impossible to do that without crossing over a high ridge and then dropping down into the canyon. The previous landowner welcomed hikers but with a change in ownership, there has been a change in access.

The best option now is to visit the head instead of the mouth of the canyon. Obtaining a forest map from the U.S. Forest Service is your best option to get directions, as you will not be traveling on major roads. Travel south on N.M. 147 into the forest and past Queen. A few miles south of Queen, turn left onto Cougar Road, also known as Forest Road 412. A short distance later, turn right onto Forest Road 540 and go about a mile to the end of the improved section of the road, an all-weather gravel road, where there is a stock tank and windmill. From here check your map for several access routes into the upper reaches of Big Canyon. The best way I've found is to drop into one of the upper reaches until the canyon joins with another one and then head back up that canyon to the top. There are many options available based on your time and capabilities to hike this area.

Big Canyon has some great wilderness values (even though it is not yet designated as wilderness), including a cliff almost 800 feet high with a Peregrine falcon nest, stands of Rocky Mountain maple in the canyon bottom, springs and tinajas, a large grotto and many caves. On the horizon to the east, at the top of one of the ridges, are found the "teeth," several large separated columns of limestone that look like teeth with spacing. The canyon is rich in plant and animal communities, and some species are found nowhere else in New Mexico. A small resident black bear population numbers less than a dozen in the entire mountain range. Rare hummingbirds and beetles add to the mix along with more than 15 plant species that are rare or endangered.

Big Canyon is a great place to get away from it all. But be careful of rattlesnakes and pending storms, and carry plenty of water. Be aware of where to put you feet and hands because of the rattlesnakes and because a sprained ankle here could be serious. But most of all, enjoy a forgotten corner of New Mexico and realize the Guadalupes are more than just a range of low hills on the horizon.

LEFT: USFS/LINCOLN NATIONAL FOREST

NM WILD STAR VOLUNTEER

Don Heinze

BY EMMA TOMINGAS-HATCH

Don Heinze has been a volunteer botanist with the New Mexico Wilderness Alliance (NM Wild) for almost three years. After retiring from the Bureau of Land Management in Billings, Montana, in 1995, he moved to Oregon but found he could not abide the frequent rain and gray skies. So, he moved to the land of the sun, New Mexico, where he joined the Native Plant Society.

Having had an interest in weeds since taking a course in college entitled, "Weeds and Poisonous Plants," he was quickly nominated to represent the Native Plant Society on the U.S. Department of Agriculture's Weed Advisory Committee.

Unfortunately, Heinze explained, weeds are very much ignored by most people until they cannot ignore them any longer. Heinze has faced a lot of apathy when it comes to his lifelong fight against noxious weeds, and he hopes that by continuing his work with the Native Plant Society and volunteering with NM Wild he can educate people about the importance of being aware of noxious weeds and invasive plants.

When NM Wild staff member Lynne Uhring contacted the Native Plant Society looking for expertise on invasive plants and weeds in 2011,

they immediately put her in touch with Heinze. Heinze was thrilled to find an organization that not only cared about noxious weeds but wanted to do something about the problem.

Heinze first began helping NM Wild by identifying invasive plants for wilderness inventories of the National Forest Service lands. He went out of his way to educate the volunteers and staff about invasive plants by creating a guide to the different types of noxious weeds in New Mexico, complete with photos. He also planned and executed a trip to the University of New Mexico Herbarium to let interested NM Wild affiliates see the plants in real life.

When the National Forest Service offered to fund the pulling of cheatgrass, a noxious weed that grows all over New Mexico, Uhring organized the service projects and Heinze was eager to help. He has gone on more than a few hikes and has actively pulled tons of cheatgrass out of the ground. He has also made himself available for any questions about the weed and has made sure that it is being identified correctly by NM Wild.

Heinze jokes that he is busier since he retired than he ever was when he was working full time. One of his main pursuits these days is working on a book for identifying noxious weeds across New Mexico. Every plant will have a two-page spread complete with a drawing and a photo to ensure the reader is identifying the weeds correctly. He is looking forward to finishing it; however, he admits that fighting against noxious weeds is not something he is doing to get rich. He is writing his book out of his love of botany and the hope that people will begin to see how important the identification and eradication of noxious weeds is to the future of our state.

When asked what his favorite thing about being an NM Wild volunteer was, Heinze smiled and said it is nice to feel like he is finally reaching people about the danger of noxious weeds and educating them on the importance of being aware of these plants in order to prevent future problems. ❁

DON HEINZE, botanist and NM Wild volunteer
His favorite wild area to go for a hike: The Sacramento Mountains. Heinze calls them the "New Mexico Galapagos" because of all the plants and animals that are considered rare and hard to find in other places.

Sandia Mountain Wilderness

BY TINA DEINES

YEAR ESTABLISHED: 1978

DESCRIPTION: The Sandia Mountain Wilderness towers above nearby Albuquerque, spanning 37,877 acres. This area is part of Cibola National Forest, which is managed by the U.S. Forest Service.

This wilderness area is home to an abundance of wildlife including mule deer, black bear, raccoon, bobcat, rattlesnake, ringtail and various species of squirrel. Several birds of prey also live in and migrate to the Sandia Mountain Wilderness, including the golden eagle, falcon and several species of hawk. Also seen here are New Mexico's state bird—the roadrunner, Steller's jay, ravens and canyon wrens. Fauna includes fir and spruce trees. Ponderosas and conifers are present in the middle elevations.

The Sandia Mountain Wilderness is well known for its tramway—one of the longest in the world. The tram spans 2.7 miles in length and gains nearly 4,000 feet in elevation to reach the crest of the Sandias. Once on top, there are various trails to choose from, including the Crest Trail, which runs along 26.54 miles of the main ridge of the Sandias at an elevation that averages 10,000 feet. Altogether, the Sandia Mountain Wilderness has around 117 miles of maintained trails.

Backcountry camping is permitted in the Sandia Mountains outside of picnic areas. Occasionally backcountry travel is prohibited due to fire danger. For more information, contact the Sandia Ranger District.

Because of its close proximity to Albuquerque, the Sandia Mountain Wilderness gets some of the most traffic of any wilderness area in the

state. While this certainly makes it more difficult to find solitude, it is not impossible to enjoy a quiet hike by yourself. On popular trails such as the Pino Trail, Embudo Trail and Three Gun Spring Trail, expect to pass by a few other hikers—most hikers will be found in the first half mile to mile from the trailhead, however. You can also try hiking during non-peak hours (such as weekdays) to enjoy a quieter hike.

WEATHER AND PRECAUTIONS:
The Sandia Mountain Wilderness contains desert and has few access points to water. In the summer, come prepared for hot conditions by bringing a hat and wearing light reflective clothing. During all seasons, remember to bring plenty of water and sunscreen.

DIRECTIONS:
The Sandia Mountain Wilderness is adjacent to several towns and cities, with the largest being Albuquerque to the west. Access to many of the trails can be gained from the Albuquerque foothills.

CONTACT:
Sandia Ranger District
11776 Hwy 337
Tijeras, NM 87059
505-281-3304
www.fs.usda.gov/cibola

Crest Trail

LEVEL: Difficult
LENGTH: 26.5 miles
ELEVATION CHANGE: 4,118 ft.
ACCESS TO TRAILHEAD: The south trailhead is accessible from Interstate 40, exit 175. Go under the interstate and turn right on the paved road through the Canyon Estates subdivision. To access the trail from the north end, take Forest Road 231 south of N.M. 165 to Tunnel Spring in Placitas.
DESCRIPTION: Because of the length and range of elevations found in the Crest Trail, this trail hosts more diverse wildlife, plants and geology than any other trail in the Sandia Mountains.

Three Gun Spring Trail

LEVEL: Moderate
LENGTH: 4 miles
ELEVATION CHANGE: 2,133 ft.
ACCESS TO TRAILHEAD: Take Interstate 40 to exit 170 and continue east on N.M. 333 for 1.5 miles until you reach the Monticello subdivision. There will be a series of signs leading you toward the trailhead.
DESCRIPTION: This trail offers great panoramic views and travels through the Upper Sonoran life zone. The lower part of the trail has little tree cover, making it an excellent choice for winter hiking.

ADDITIONAL RESOURCES:
Field Guide to the Sandia Mountains, edited by Robert Julyan and Mary Stuever

Explore Together

Experience some of the Land of Enchantment's most **kid-friendly outdoor hikes**

BY JULIA QUINTANA

Hiking in the Land of Enchantment is a great way to keep kids active and healthy and can be a bonding experience for the entire family. For those families with busy schedules, day hikes may be a more practical approach to the outdoors. Here are some fun kid-friendly hikes around New Mexico that are sure to expose your kids to the history and beauty of the state.

ALBUQUERQUE AREA- Manzano Mountains

If you are looking for a fun day hike near Albuquerque, the Fourth of July Trailhead and Campground in the Manzano Mountains is a colorful place to start. The best season to explore this area is autumn, when multitudes of maple trees turn brilliant shades of scarlet. The trail climbs past a spring and ends in a meadow with breathtaking views. This hike is great for kids because it follows a gentle path within a shady canyon and offers fantastic views and opportunities to collect maple leaves.

NORTHERN NEW MEXICO- San Pedro Parks Wilderness

The San Pedro Parks Wilderness, just east of Cuba, is another excellent place for a family hike. The Vacas Trail passes through a spruce-fir forest for a mile until it reaches the San Gregorio Reservoir. This is the perfect place to stop for a picnic and admire the scenery. The trail eventually connects with the Clear Creek Trail, where it is common to see a variety of fungi, plant life and the occasional elk. Due to its isolated location, this area is less heavily traveled and serves as an ideal spot for a peaceful getaway.

SILVER CITY AREA- The Gila Cliff Dwellings National Monument

The Gila Cliff Dwellings National Monument, located north of Silver City in the Gila National Forest, is a must-see destination for children of all ages. Children under 16 gain free admission to the monument, where they have access to the visitor center and the Junior Ranger Program. The West Fork Trail is a one-mile loop that grants fabulous views of the cave dwellings, which once housed the ancient Mogollon people. The Middle Fork Trail stays at river level, passing several hot springs. Both trails offer kids a great opportunity to learn about history and explore scenic landscapes.

MORGUEFILE.COM

SOUTHEAST NEW MEXICO-
Smokey Bear Historical Park

While not a "hike" in itself, Smokey Bear Historical Park is a great place to bring kids to learn about one of New Mexico's most famous historical figures, Smokey Bear. The visitor center features exhibits about forest health, forest fires, wildland/urban interface issues and fire ecology. There is also a playground, picnic area and outdoor amphitheater. The park participates in the Junior Ranger and Little Ranger programs—children between 7 and 12 years old can complete a workbook to earn a patch, certificate and membership card to the Junior Ranger Program while younger children can earn a comic book and sticker for completing a worksheet.

Gila Wilderness

BY MARK ALLISON

YEAR ESTABLISHED: 1964 (Included in the Wilderness Act) and expanded in 1980
1924 (America's—and the world's—first administratively designated wilderness)

DESCRIPTION: I'm biased. I'm smitten. I admit it. The Gila Wilderness is one of my first loves and still among my very favorite places. It is big. Really big. It is wild. Really wild. It can swallow up a week-long backpack trip without a second thought. And because many Burqueños and Santa Feans seem to automatically (and unfairly) write off anything south of Interstate 40 when we scratch the itch to get outside, the Gila is empty. Really empty. Running water, warm springs, dipping vats, cliff dwellings and wildlife galore—including wolves—make it that much more special. And the history—walking in the footsteps of Geronimo and Aldo Leopold—c'mon!

The Gila Wilderness is 557,873 acres, making it one of the largest roadless areas in the lower 48 (the adjacent Aldo Leopold Wilderness in the Black Range is an additional 202,016 acres). The beautiful Gila River is one of the last wild, free-flowing rivers in the Southwest—though currently under threat from an unnecessary and ill-conceived diversion plan.

Gila River Middle Fork

ANN McMAHON ©2012

Whether you want to camp with the family, backpack with your buddies or fish or hunt by yourself, the Gila has opportunities to explore for a lifetime. Birders and wildlife watchers will not be disappointed. Going for a short after-dinner walk around my campsite while solo backpacking one year, I shared a quiet frozen moment with the biggest bull elk I've ever seen, not 30 yards away, his rack so enormous I still can't

Gila Area Photographer Supports Wilderness

Ann McMahon
www.AnnMcMahon.com

Since her move to Silver City in 2011, photographer **Ann McMahon** has worked steadily to produce portfolios of Southwest New Mexico and Gila area images for the opening of her gallery in Silver City as part of the Silver City Gallery Association Red Dot Tours. McMahon has been a photographer since 1970, producing calendars, note cards, brochures, prints and other publications for companies and organizations. As part of her commercial work and as a pilot, McMahon has used her knowledge of aviation to produce aerial images. She has studied fine art printing with Charles Cramer for 10 years and is putting her skills to work producing fine art prints of the Southwest New Mexico landscape and animals. She is working with NM Wild to produce photos for upcoming print and Web publications.

fathom how he navigated the trees when he finally snorted and bounded away. Those more interested in geology or archaeology will also be pleased.

There are hundreds of miles of maintained hiking trails traversing river valleys, canyons, grassy Ponderosa pine parklands and mountain tops. Nearby campgrounds provide convenient staging areas for multi-day trips into the interior. The Gila is so large and so diverse, there is something for everybody.

WEATHER AND PRECAUTIONS:
This is remote country with varied terrain including deep canyons and steep mountains. The Gila can be enjoyed any time of year, though as expected, winters can be very cold, particularly at higher elevations, and the canyon floors can be quite hot during the summer months. The mountains can have heavy snowpack in certain years, sometimes extending into May or even June. Call ahead if traveling in the winter to make sure certain roads are open. No matter what time of year, take appropriate clothing and dress in layers.

Some trails have numerous river crossings, which can be difficult or impassable during spring snowmelts or after monsoon rains. Away from the river corridors, water is scarce and you will either need to pack in what you need or be absolutely confident of locations and flows of spring-fed sources.

DIRECTIONS:
The Gila Wilderness is a vast stretch of land covering approximately 40 miles east to west and 30 miles north to south, not including adjacent and nearby national forest lands. Most visitors gain access to the wilderness via N.M. 15 that runs north from Silver City, via U.S. 180 and access points out of Glenwood or via N.M. 12 out of Apache Creek or Reserve. There are other possibilities depending on where you are going—consult a New Mexico back roads atlas.

CONTACT:
Gila National Forest
3005 E. Camino del Bosque
Silver City, NM 88061-7863
575-388-8201

For more information, read *Hiking New Mexico's Gila Wilderness* by Bill Cunningham and Polly Burke.

BUREAU OF LAND MANAGEMENT

"Ethical behavior is doing the right thing when no one else is watching—even when doing the wrong thing is legal."

—Aldo Leopold

Wilderness Stewardship

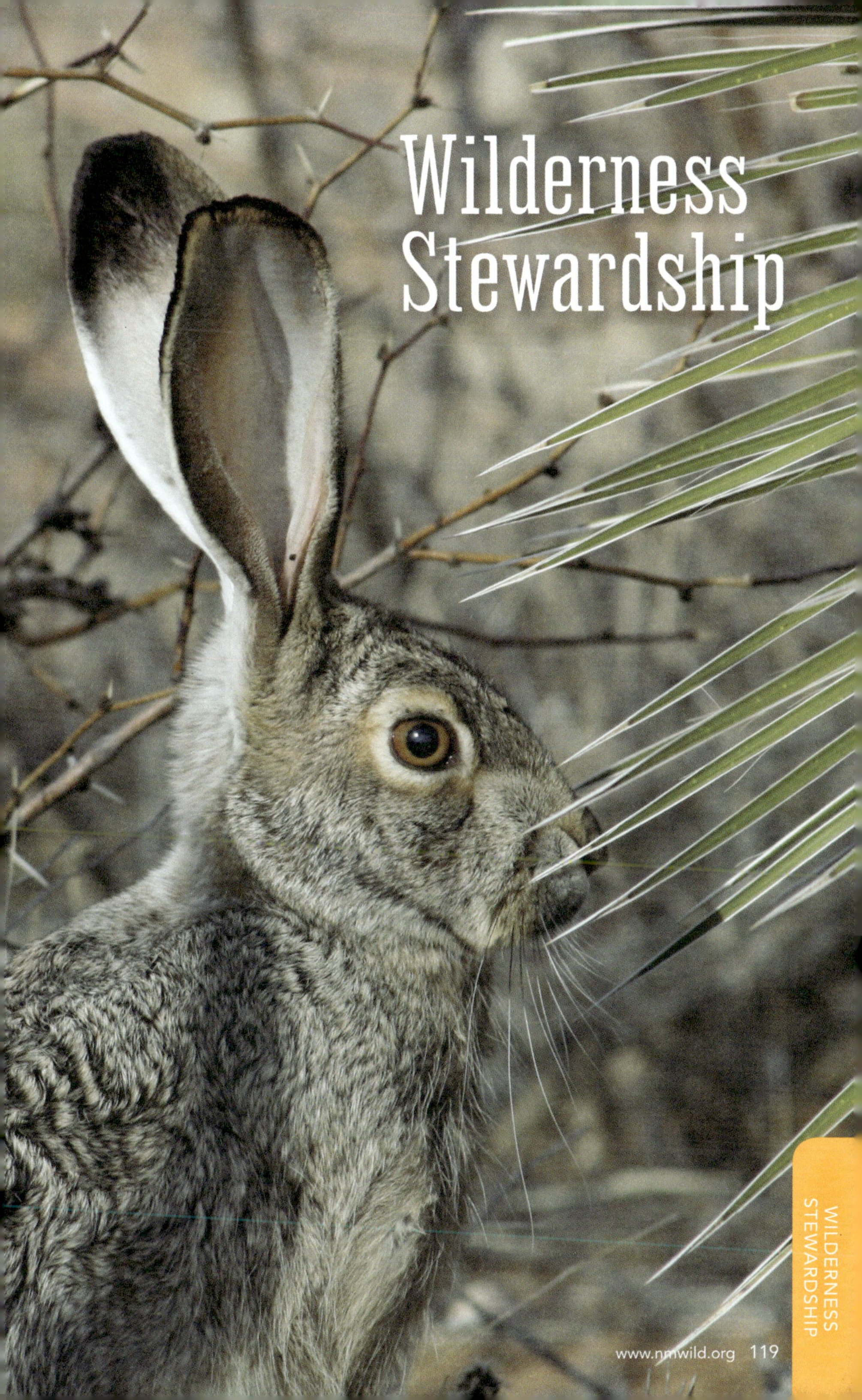

New Mexico on FIRE

BY TINA DEINES

BUREAU OF LAND MANAGEMENT

Fire is a very real concern here in New Mexico and the entire West, especially during a drought. In the past few years, the state has endured major fires in the Gila Wilderness, the Pecos Wilderness and the White Mountain Wilderness. We can't prevent all wildfires, but shockingly, **nine out of 10 wildfires are caused by humans**. While enjoying the outdoors in New Mexico it is crucial to keep fire safety in mind.

EXTINGUISHING YOUR CAMPFIRE

(from www.smokeybear.com)

- Allow the wood to burn completely to ash, if possible.
- Pour lots of water on the fire to drown ALL embers, not just the red ones.
- Pour until hissing sound stops.
- Stir the campfire ashes and embers with a shovel.
- Scrape the sticks and logs to remove any embers.
- Stir and make sure everything is wet and cold to the touch.
- If you do not have water, use dirt. Mix enough dirt or sand with the embers. Continue adding and stirring until all material is cool. Remember: Do NOT bury the fire as it will continue to smolder and could catch roots on fire that will eventually get to the surface and start a wildfire.

More information about campfire

safety can be found online at: *www.smokeybear.com/campfire-safety.asp*. Please also be aware of fire restrictions in your area. Remember, you don't have to be building a big campfire to violate fire restrictions—even smoking a cigarette outside may be prohibited during Stage II fire restrictions. Fire restrictions and closure information can be found by calling 877-864-6985 or going online to *http://firerestrictions.us/nm.*

SMOKEY'S STORY

Smokey Bear isn't just a cartoon image. In 1950, a fire erupted in the Capitan Mountains Wilderness of New Mexico. As crews worked together to fight for control of this raging fire, they discovered a lonely bear cub wandering near the fire line. Initially, they left the cub alone, thinking that its mother was nearby. However, the cub became caught in the path of the fire, taking refuge in a tree. When crews found him in the tree, he was badly burned on his paws and hind legs. Soldiers removed the cub from the tree, and a local rancher agreed to take him home. Soon, the 5-pound cub was on his way to Santa Fe where his burns were treated and bandaged at Smith Veterinary Hospital, still today one of Santa Fe's oldest family-owned businesses. News of the courageous little bear hit the press nationwide, and many people called and wrote to find out more about his progress. The cub was presented to the U.S. Forest Service to serve as an ambassador for fire prevention and conservation publicity campaigns. And so it was—the little cub was sent to the National Zoo in Washington, D.C., where he served as the living symbol of Smokey Bear until he died at 26 years old. Smokey's body was returned to New Mexico and people can visit his grave at the Smokey Bear Historical Park in Capitan. See how the Smokey Bear campaign has progressed over the years: *www.smokeybear.com/vault.*

USFS/SMOKEY BEAR MUSEUM

An injured cub became the popular "spokesbear" for the National Forest Service in the 1950s.

Wilderness Stewardship

BY TISHA BROSKA, Associate Director

Desert wanderings, sinuous paths through a forest, streams of life, fields of wildflowers—wilderness offers it all. It's a place where our souls are free and our mind and body connect with nature. You know the feeling of anticipation you get when you have to hike just a little bit farther to see what is around the next bend or just a little higher up trail to get a better view? The sense of adventure we get walking and exploring the wilderness comes from freedom. You feel as though no other person may have been in this part of the earth before, even though thousands may have walked this path before you. You have freedom in your connection to the wild.

Being in the wilderness, away from the constant pull of our always-connected and overly busy daily lives, forces us to make a different kind of connection, one much more primal and meaningful—the connection to nature. This connection offers all of us spiritual renewal.

"We need the tonic of wildness... At the same time that we are earnest to explore and learn all things, we require that all things be mysterious and unexplorable, that land and sea be indefinitely wild, unsurveyed and unfathomed by us because unfathomable. We can never have enough of nature," Henry David Thoreau wrote in *Walden: Or, Life in the Woods*.

America's National Wilderness Preservation System is unsurpassed the world over, made up of nearly 110 million acres of wild public lands (see pages 38-69). Many visitors to wilderness areas are profoundly touched by the freedom they find and the experiences held in wild places. Most agree that our best wild public lands should be preserved so that future generations are able to enjoy these sacred places, just as they have been passed down to us.

Wilderness stewardship can mean many things. It may be closely related to how an area is managed to accommodate people and wildlife. Stewardship can also involve working to restore wounds to the land or restore native plants and wildlife. For the New Mexico Wilderness Alliance

> "Like music and art, love of nature is a common language that can transcend political or social boundaries."
> — Jimmy Carter

(NM Wild), stewardship is also about permanently protecting more of our wild public lands while we still can. Today, only 2 percent of New Mexico is permanently protected. Simply put, keeping the land whole, wild and free is one of the most important aspects of responsibly caring for our lands. Wallace Stegner may have said it best: "The best thing we have learned from nearly 500 years of contact with the American wilderness is restraint, the willingness to hold our hand: to visit such places for our soul's good, but to leave no tracks."

In addition to protecting, managing and restoring the land for wilderness character, stewardship is also about teaching a land ethic. We must teach respect for nature to foster the future stewards of the wilderness we work so hard to protect and restore. Because, truly, as the saying goes, "We do not inherit the earth from our ancestors; we borrow it from our children." Yet we must all work to turn those who will inherit the earth from us into stewards.

We can all be stewards of the land. A simple hike can become an exercise in stewardship by following Leave No Trace principles and teaching them to children. We also can be stewards in our everyday lives by picking up trash, documenting invasive non-native plants or advocating for additional wilderness protection. By taking time to respect the land and teach others the values our wild lands hold for our clean air, clean water and wildlife, we pass on a land ethic that will include wilderness.

You can partner with NM Wild by joining us on a volunteer service project. We conduct more than 40 guided hikes and restoration projects each year. From wildlife monitoring to inventorying lands for wilderness characteristics to identifying and removing invasive plants, we have a project for you. Each year our volunteers contribute about 8,000 hours of volunteer time during hands-on stewardship projects and hikes.

You Can Help – Learn More About Stewardship

A good place to start is the website and programs of the Leave No Trace Center (*www.LNT.org*), a world leader in teaching minimum impact skills to adults and young people. Additional information can be found at wilderness.net. Contact local wilderness managers for other ideas promoting stewardship.

In 2014, we celebrate the 50th anniversary of the Wilderness Act, which defines wilderness as a place "Where the earth and its community of life are untrammeled by man," and mandates that preserving the wilderness character is the primary goal in the management of wilderness areas. See page 73 for more information about this event.

DRAGONFLY: BUREAU OF LAND MANAGEMENT
BUTTERFLY: USFS/LINCOLN NATIONAL FOREST

VIEW FROM ABOVE

New Mexico Wilderness Alliance campaign staff members often join with **LightHawk** to take our political delegation, local reporters and other groups on flights over our campaign areas. LightHawk is a volunteer-based aviation organization with more than 200 volunteer pilots. The group provides flights as a tool to protect land, water and wildlife in the U.S., Mexico, Central America and parts of Canada. In 2013, we took flights over the proposed Columbine Hondo Wilderness, Rio Grande del Norte National Monument and the proposed Organ Mountains-Desert Peaks National Monument. Trips such as these are part of our mission to work with diverse supporters to encourage the protection of our campaign areas across the state. Learn more about LightHawk: *www.lighthawk.org*

Ute Mountain

LEFT: JOHN OLIVAS; RIGHT: NATHAN SMALL

JOHN OLIVAS
Rio Grande Gorge Bridge

JEFF STEINBORN
Lighthawk aircraft near Organ Mountains

Historic WWII bombing targets in the Sierra de las Uvas Mountains, northwest of Las Cruces

WILDERNESS STEWARDSHIP CHALLENGE

Sandia Mountain Wilderness
Non-native Invasive Plant Monitoring and Removal Project

JUNE 2012 TO JUNE 2013

BY LYNNE UHRING

In partnership with the National Forest Foundation, the New Mexico Wilderness Alliance (NM Wild) has been assisting the Sandia Ranger District of the Cibola National Forest in battling invasive plants. Since June of 2012, we have been training volunteers and organizing volunteer service projects to monitor and remove non-native invasive plants. The main culprit is cheatgrass.

Cheatgrass (*Bromus tectorum L.*) is a highly invasive annual grass. It was likely brought to North America in the 1800s from the Mediterranean with domestic animals and livestock feed. Because it has no natural enemies in North America to deter its growth, it spreads rapidly, crowding out the natural vegetation. It starts growing early in the spring, taking the moisture out of the soil before the native grasses get a chance to germinate. Once it starts growing, it rapidly produces seeds, thus having another advantage over the slower-growing native grasses. Cheatgrass earned its name because of its poor nutritional value—its seeds have about half the nutritional value of the seeds of native grasses. Native birds and small mammals that eat seeds are "cheated" out of the more nutritious native seeds.

Irene Walkiw

LEFT & RIGHT: LYNNE UHRING

Jackie Ericksen

More than 100 volunteers recorded more than 1,000 hours training, monitoring and removing cheatgrass in the wilderness. Don Heinze (read more about Don on pages 110-111), a retired botanist and invasive plant

WIKIMEDIA COMMONS

Cheatgrass earned its name because of its poor nutritional value—its seeds have about half the nutritional value of the seeds of native grasses.

specialist, donated professional volunteer hours conducting workshops, preparing plant identification sheets and educating volunteers. We'd like to give special thanks to stalwart volunteers Irene Walkiw and Jackie Ericksen and to Kristian Mueller, an NM Wild GIS intern from the University of New Mexico, who contributed greatly to the cheatgrass project during 2013.

Since 2012, cheatgrass has been recorded with geocoded photographs in 72 distinct locations, mostly on the west side of the Sandia Mountains. If the cheatgrass seeds are still green, we pull the plant to prevent formation of new seeds and can leave it behind. The green seeds will not mature. If the seeds are brown, then we must pull the plant and carry it out so that those mature seeds will not germinate the next season. Other non-native plants identified were Siberian elm, Tree of Heaven and thistle.

A detailed map of the work done in the Sandia Mountain Wilderness for this project can be found at *www.nmwild.org/2013/news/wilderness-stewardship-challenge-homepage*.
To find out about volunteer projects in national forest wilderness areas during 2014, contact Lynne Uhring at *lynne@nmwild.org* or 505-843-8696, ext 110.

In 2012, NM Wild conducted wilderness inventories in the Lincoln National Forest, including the Capitan Wilderness pictured here, and the White Mountain Wilderness.

LYNNE UHRING

Protecting Our Land THROUGH Wilderness Inventories

BY LYNNE UHRING

If you are a New Mexico Wilderness Alliance (NM Wild) supporter, you have heard about Otero Mesa. Forests of 20-foot-tall yucca interrupt vast expanses of open prairie. Pronghorn antelope flash through 50-mile vistas. Evenings and mornings thrill with the sights and sounds of migrating birds. The nights burst with stars, stillness and silence. Visitors might meet another human, but more often no one else is there. Otero Mesa is wilderness in the truest, wildest sense.

Early in 2013, the BLM released its Draft Revised Management Plan for Doña Ana, Sierra and Otero counties. In that management plan, the agency recognized only 803 acres as having wilderness potential—none of the acres was in Otero County.

In March 2012, the BLM released a detailed manual outlining the criteria for determining if an area

Completing inventories across the state and creating maps is an ongoing project that helps us advise federal agencies.

qualifies as "Lands with Wilderness Characteristics." Armed with maps developed from NM Wild's extensive field work done 10 years before and GPS mobile camera devices, NM Wild staff members and eight hearty volunteers headed out to collect new field data following the BLM manual.

Over the course of a year, spending more than 25 days and nights in the field, staff and volunteers collected 750 geocoded photographs that documented 31 different areas totaling 356,000 acres of potential Lands with Wilderness Characteristics. Volunteers collected 35 percent of the data points and contributed 180 hours of work.

Back at the NM Wild office in Albuquerque, the ever-growing body of raw field data was edited and added to the geographic information system (GIS) map. From the main database, maps and photographs for each of the 31 proposed wilderness areas were grouped into individual unit proposals. Our hard-earned field data, photographs and maps were submitted in September 2013 to the BLM as citizens' input demonstrating that Otero Mesa meets the BLM's own definition of Lands with Wilderness Characteristics.

Our GIS/mapping program is one important aspect of NM Wild's commitment to protecting our best public lands. Completing inventories across the state and creating maps is an ongoing project that helps us advise federal agencies and develop our own wilderness campaigns.

PAULA EASTWOOD

Mobile GIS data collection unit

THE PRINCIPLES OF

LEAVING NO TRACE

Leave what you find—
potsherds near Abiquiú.

Wilderness is especially important to the history, culture and future of New Mexico. New Mexico was the birthplace of wilderness with the Gila Wilderness.

Our public lands are the foundation of our state and still offer the beauty and naturalness that make New Mexico the Land of Enchantment. With a changing society that is more mobile and more connected than ever, our public lands have never been more important than they are today.

New Mexico Wilderness Alliance strives to connect New Mexicans of all ages to our public lands to teach them the value of wilderness. Join us for a hike or volunteer service project (found on pages 38-69 of this guide) or venture out on your own.

When outdoors or on the trails, please take the time to observe and practice the seven principles of Leave No Trace to leave a minimal impact on the land:

- Plan ahead and prepare
- Travel and camp on durable surfaces
- Dispose of waste properly
- Leave what you find
- Minimize campfire impacts
- Respect wildlife
- Be considerate of other visitors

The member-driven Leave No Trace Center for Outdoor Ethics teaches people how to enjoy the outdoors responsibly. This copyrighted information has been reprinted with permission from the Leave No Trace Center for Outdoor Ethics: www.LNT.org.

BUREAU OF LAND MANAGEMENT

Steller's Jay

Check Us Out Online—visit us at nmwild.org

- Become a member
- Sign up for hikes and service projects
- Shop at our online store
- Read about our campaigns
- Get all the latest news

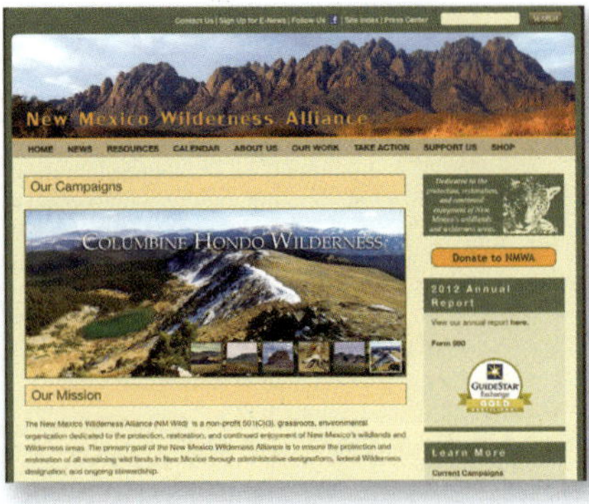

Plus, check out our social media to stay up to date on the most current happenings and to connect with us.

facebook.com/nmwilderness

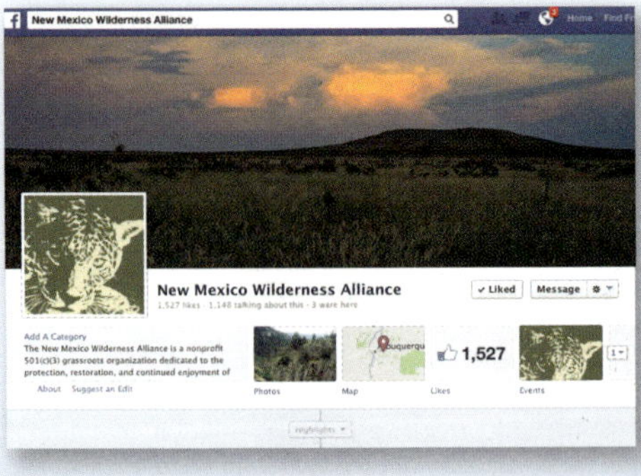

YouTube: www.youtube.com/user/TheNMWA

Twitter: www.twitter.com/nmwild

Mexican Wolf
Conservation Stamp

2013 Wolf Stamp art by Susan Miller

The stamp pictured here is not a true postage stamp—it is part of a series of framing-quality art prints offered to collectors. Order wolf stamps online at *www.nmwild.org*. Click on "Shop."

THE MEXICAN GRAY WOLF is the most endangered wolf in the world, with a total population of less than 75 in the wild.

The Mexican Wolf Conservation Stamp is a conservation project created by the New Mexico Wilderness Alliance. The concept is similar to the Duck Stamp sold by the U.S. Fish & Wildlife Service, except no hunting will be related to the sale of the stamp. Instead, proceeds will be used for the Mexican Wolf Conservation Stamp Fund, administered by NM Wild and utilized for Mexican gray wolf recovery.

NATHAN NEWCOMER

WOLF STAMP COMPETITION

Susan Miller, 2013 Wolf Stamp Winner

Artist **Susan Miller,** who is of Cherokee and European descent, was born and raised in southwestern Oklahoma and studied art at the University of North Texas. Taos is now her home, and she lives there with her husband, David, in their centuries-old adobe house. Inspired daily by the heart-stopping beauty of Northern New Mexico, Miller works primarily in acrylic, using vivid color to create large paintings on wood panels. Highly stylized wolves and coyotes are favorite subjects, along with Native American motifs inspired by her Cherokee heritage. Miller passionately supports the reintroduction of the Mexican gray wolf into the American Southwest and believes in the importance of wolves for a healthy ecosystem. "In my paintings I try to convey my love and respect for the wolf, and to honor his strong and wild spirit," she says.

"Good Wolf" by Sandra SanTara, Wolf Stamp Finalist

Sandra SanTara has been a professional visionary, wildlife and fantasy artist for more than 20 years. She has a great love of creating art with depth and meaning—focused mainly on the Shamanic, symbolic and esoteric—from flights of fantasy to realistic wildlife art. SanTara enjoys traveling and selling her work in the traditional fine art and pop culture circuits around the country. Well known nationally and internationally, she has received numerous achievement awards and is published and licensed with several well-known companies. Acrylic painting is her specialty, and painting on feathers has been the most popular of her work in that genre. Her website is: *http://windwolf.com.*

"Timeless Guardian" by Christine Graefe Drewyer, Wolf Stamp Finalist

"Painting for me is a celebration of beauty and creation and the making of art a sacred expression," says award-winning artist **Christine Drewyer.**

Drewyer has a profound love for the land and animals; it is understandable that her artistic voice expresses this passion. She is an active participant in animal conservation and protection projects and tends to focus her efforts on painting animals that are endangered in order to raise public awareness.

Drewyer is a signature member and president of Women Artists of the West as well as an active member in these fine art groups: the Washington Society of Landscape Painters, the Salmagundi Club, Oil Painters of America, American Impressionist Society, American Plains Artists and American Women Artists.

Her recent awards include the President's Award of Excellence from the Salmagundi Club and the Publishers Award of Excellence from *Art of the West* magazine.

Employer Matching Gifts Program

What's better than a personal gift to the New Mexico Wilderness Alliance? A personal gift with even more impact! You could double or triple your gift—at no extra cost to you.

You may not be aware that many companies will match their employees' donations to nonprofit organizations to significantly increase the value of an individual's charitable gift. Check with your employer to find out if they have a matching gifts program today.

DESERT SOUTHWEST COMBINED FEDERAL CAMPAIGN

The New Mexico Wilderness Alliance is proud to participate in the Desert Southwest Combined Federal Campaign. The Combined Federal Campaign (CFC) allows charitable organizations to solicit contributions from employees of the federal government of the United States. The Combined Federal Campaign is the world's largest and most successful annual workplace charity campaign.

Pledges made by employees through their paychecks support tax-exempt charities, like NM Wild. Charities that apply to receive funds through the CFC are required to submit to extensive review of their financial and governance practices prior to acceptance. This eligibility review has helped set standards for participation in giving. Of the one million charities operating in the United States today, it is estimated that fewer than 5 percent meet or exceed these standards.

NM Wild is proud to be one of them.

If you are eligible and interested in supporting NM Wild through the Desert Southwest Combined Federal Campaign, **NM Wild's charity ID number is 90043.**

Go to ***desertswcfc.org*** to pledge your support today.

CFC®
Combined Federal Campaign

Financial Rewards Waiting At
New Mexico Educators Credit Union

As a member of the New Mexico Wilderness Alliance (NM Wild), you are eligible to join New Mexico Educators Federal Credit Union. New Mexico Educators FCU is the state's largest not-for-profit financial cooperative with more than 130,000 member-owners and 16 full-service branch offices from Taos to Socorro. The credit union offers a full range of financial services at low cost or no cost. You'll find checking and savings options; mortgage, equity and auto loans; credit cards and investment services. Free Internet banking; bill payer service; iPhone, Android and iPad mobile banking apps; and mobile and text banking are available, and all members receive free identity fraud resolution service.

New Mexico Educators FCU offers two exclusive programs to reward members' economic participation –Community Rewards and Member Rewards.

Community Rewards is a program that can benefit both you and NM Wild. You can change your world, one purchase at a time—all you need to participate is a credit union checking account and a Visa® Check Card. When you enroll in Community Rewards, you select a community and category for your credit union's annual gift giving: Environment and Wildlife, Education, Healthcare, The Arts or Community Support. You will earn a 0.25 percent cash reward with every signature-based purchase you make. Then each year, New Mexico Educators FCU makes a matching contribution to your designated area of support.

Member Rewards is the money you can earn for maintaining your accounts, loans and credit cards at the credit union. The more you participate financially, the more you earn. There is no enrollment required; if you meet the eligibility criteria, you automatically earn Member Rewards. Detailed information is available at *www.nmefcu.org*.

New Mexico Educators Federal Credit Union maintains the safety and soundness principles and values that have been part of the international credit union movement for more than 200 years. BauerFinancial Inc. has ranked New Mexico Educators FCU as five stars for financial strength and security. You can join by visiting any branch (location information at *www.nmefcu.org*) or by calling 889-7755 or 800-347-2838 (outside the Albuquerque area) Monday through Saturday.

THEY TAKE.
WE REWARD.
YOU DO THE MATH.
$
With some banks, it's all take, take, take. It doesn't have to be like that. At New Mexico Educators Federal Credit Union, you can be rewarded for your participation. Add it up yourself. Go to nmefcu.org to calculate your potential rewards.
SCAN THIS QR CODE OR VISIT NMEFCU.ORG
NEW MEXICO EDUCATORS FEDERAL CREDIT UNION
The Power of WE.
16 Branch Locations from Socorro to Taos
505-889-7755 • 800-347-2838 • nmefcu.org
Federally insured by NCUA

How to Pack a Backpack

From the American Hiking Society *www.americanhiking.org*

A correctly organized backpack will make your hike even more comfortable. Regardless of how in shape you might be, incorrectly packing a backpack can quickly lead to overexertion on even the simplest of hikes. Here are a few tips to make your backpack as comfortable as possible. Keep in mind, however, this is a general guideline. You may have to tweak these tips a little bit depending on what gear you decide to bring on a hike.

FIND THE RIGHT BACKPACK. First things first: Be sure that your backpack fits you well and also will be adequate for your hike. If you are going on a simple day hike, you don't need a humongous expedition pack. Likewise, daypacks are generally too small for multi-day use.

SLEEPING BAG AT THE BOTTOM. Even though most hikers will build upon these general rules to create their unique packing system, almost everyone agrees that your sleeping bag belongs at the bottom of the pack. On an external frame pack, this means it is lashed to the frame below the pack itself.

BACK BREAKERS. Heavier items should be kept close to your back and higher up in your pack to help you maintain a center of gravity. This setup keeps you from breaking your back with heavy loads that pull your pack backwards or side to side. Avoid skewing the weight distribution to one side. Even complex suspension systems on internal frame packs can't compensate for a dramatic difference in weight from one side to another.

PLAN FOR EASY ACCESS. Put essential items like a map, first-aid kit, flashlight and trail snacks on outside pouches or in upper compartments for easy access during breaks. Many packs have holsters or mesh side-pockets for your water bottles. Other items like spare clothing or a ground cloth that you know you won't use until you get to a campsite should be deeper in your pack.

DON'T WASTE SPACE! Cram your cooking pots with food or your stove so they don't get separated. If you put extra clothing in a re-sealable plastic bag to keep it dry, squeeze the air out of the bag before completely zipping it up.

PREVENT FOOD AND GEAR SPOILAGE. Fuel for your stove should be nowhere near your food or your tent. Double check the cap to ensure it is screwed on tightly. Leaky fuel can spoil your food and ruin the waterproof layers of your tent or raingear.

WATERPROOF YOUR PACK. A good pack cover will not just keep the contents of your pack dry but will also keep the pack itself dry. Water is heavy, so a dry pack is nice on many levels. Still, it's a good idea to put your clothing and any electronics in re-sealable plastic bags to ensure it all stays dry. Alternatively, you could line the inside of your backpack with a plastic trash bag. A stuff sack with a down sleeping bag should be lined with a plastic bag, especially if it is on the outside of a pack. Down sleeping bags must be completely dry to be effective.

MORGUEFILE.COM

IF YOU USE AN EXTERNAL FRAME PACK, you may have to lash several items to the outside of the pack. Tie each item down as tightly as possible so that it doesn't sway as you walk. The extra movement on the pack will make you work harder to keep your balance on the trail. Overall, try to minimize the number of items you keep on the outside of your pack.

WEAR YOUR PACK CORRECTLY. When putting on your pack, loosen all the straps. First tighten the hip belt (which should be on your hips, not above them), then the shoulder straps and then the load lifters (near your shoulders). Finally adjust the load stabilizer straps on the hip belt (at the back of the belt). Your sternum strap should not be tight but simply help keep the shoulder straps in position—you want to be able to breathe freely.

This list is just a general guide to help you find out what works best for you. With practice and experience you'll find a packing method that best suits the equipment you prefer to take with you on your hikes. ❁

NM Wild would like to thank our
2013 Online Auction Sponsors!

LOBO LEVEL SPONSORS ($500 AND UP)

Budd Berkman
Doctors Judy Lui and Julian Rowe
Avocet Design and Consulting
Mesilla Abodes
Robin Jackson Photography
Filson
Marcello's Chophouse
Diane Bloom

PRONGHORN LEVEL SPONSORS ($250-$499)

David Soules
High Desert Birding
Ken and Jane Cole
Rio Grande Soaring Association
Sorenson's Inn
Deborah Donelson Art
Bishop's Lodge Ranch Resort and Spa
The Inn at Vanessie
Cashmere Rouge Spa
La Provence
Cottonwood Gulch
Mike Roussel, DMD
Hotel Andaluz
The Curious Kumquat

ROADRUNNER LEVEL SPONSORS ($100-$249)

Aletta Lawrence
Lu Mellado, phetishes
Sandra SanTara Art
Wild Earth Llama Adventures
Robert Marchand
General Palmer Hotel
Ruffwear
The Strater Hotel
Cumbres and Toltec Scenic Railroad
Black Diamond
STM Bags
Sara Jayne Cole
Skarsgard Farms
Whole Foods, Indian School-Albuquerque
La Fonda Hotel
Hyatt Regency, Albuquerque
Cutting Edge, Regina Klapper
Storm Sermay Photography
Robert Villegas Photography
Kate Mott
Joan Zalenski

What Would You Like Your Legacy to Be?

Are you passionate about the wild landscapes and wildlife of New Mexico? Do you want to be sure that nature is preserved for generations to come? Your legacy gift to the New Mexico Wilderness Alliance (NM Wild) will ensure that the wilderness, wildlife and water of the Land of Enchantment are protected forever.

Become a New Mexico Wilderness Alliance Steward today.

If you are planning to create a new will or update an existing one, we hope you will consider a future gift to protect and safeguard New Mexico's wilderness, water and wildlife. NM Wild Stewards are individuals who have included a future gift to NM Wild through their will or estate plans. Becoming a NM Wild Steward can be as simple as including a bequest to our organization in your will or designating our organization as one of the beneficiaries of a retirement plan or life insurance policy.

Please contact me if you would like to include NM Wild in your will or retirement plan.

Tisha Broska
505-843-8696 ext.106
tisha@nmwild.org
www.nmwild.org/support-us/legacy

Do you donate to the United Way through your employer?
Ask that your gift be directed to the New Mexico Wilderness Alliance to help support our work.

Does your employer have a donation-matching program?
Your donation to New Mexico Wilderness Alliance could be eligible for matching donations from your work.

New Mexico Wilderness Alliance
www.nmwild.org

Yes! I would like to support New Mexico wilderness!

Contributions are tax deductible to the full extent of the law.
Go to *www.nmwild.org* to make your donation online today!

YES! I support the efforts of New Mexico Wilderness Alliance.
ENCLOSED IS MY GIFT OF:

- ❑ $25
- ❑ $50
- ❑ $100
- ❑ $500
- ❑ $750
- ❑ $1,000
- ❑ Other $__________
- ❑ Sign me up for Monthly Giving. I pledge $__________ per month, charged to my credit card.
- ❑ Please send me information on making a bequest to New Mexico Wilderness Alliance.

Name____________________
Address____________________
City, State, Zip____________________
E-mail: ____________________
Phone:____________________

PAYMENT OPTIONS

- ❑ Enclosed is my check payable to New Mexico Wilderness Alliance, PO Box 25464, Abq, NM 87125
- ❑ Please charge my Visa, Mastercard, AmEx, Discover (circle one)

Card #: ____________________
Exp. Date: ____________________
Signature: ____________________

GIVE a gift membership to the NEW MEXICO WILDERNESS ALLIANCE!
Please send a Gift Membership to:

Name____________________
Address____________________
City, State, Zip____________________

Yucca plant in Chihuahuan desert

USFS/LINCOLN NATIONAL FOREST